This admirably accessible introduction to 'the basics' of ELT provides a review of key elements of English language teaching that is ideally suited to trainee teachers and those early in their career. Drawing on the authors' wide-ranging knowledge and expertise, this informative text combines real world data with reflective tasks as it outlines key elements of language teaching and learning. With its suggestions for further reading and discussion of pathways for professional development, it provides an excellent overview for those starting out in ELT.

Graham Hall, Northumbria University, UK

ELT

THE BASICS

ELT: The Basics offers a clear, non-jargonistic introduction to English language teaching for EFL/ESL teachers in training, early career teachers, those considering taking up ELT, and experienced teachers who may want to read about the way the profession has developed and continues to evolve.

Key features of this book include:

- Real classroom data and data from ELT training programmes
- Discussion of a wide range of learning contexts and different types of learners (young learners, adults, third age, academic, refugees and immigrants, etc.)
- Comparisons of different types of syllabuses and methods, and discussion of current technologies
- An emphasis on classroom interaction as the key to maximising learning

Featuring a glossary of key terms, cartoons and illustrations, further reading, personal reflection points, and discussion of the most important and relevant research, this book is a clear and accessible introduction to the complex field of ELT.

Michael McCarthy is Emeritus Professor of Applied Linguistics, University of Nottingham, UK, and Honorary Professor of Applied Linguistics, University of Valencia, Spain. He has (co-)authored and edited 60 books and was co-founder (with Ronald Carter) of the CANCODE spoken English corpus. He has lectured in 46 countries and has been involved in language teaching and applied linguistics for 57 years.

Steve Walsh is Professor of Applied Linguistics and Communication, School of Education, Communication and Language Sciences, Newcastle University, UK. He is also a visiting professor at the University of Hong Kong. He has published 10 books and more than 100 research papers. He has been involved in English language teaching and English language teacher education for more than 30 years in a range of overseas contexts.

The Basics

The Basics is a highly successful series of accessible guidebooks which provide an overview of the fundamental principles of a subject area in a jargon-free and undaunting format. Intended for students approaching a subject for the first time, the books both introduce the essentials of a subject and provide an ideal springboard for further study. With over 50 titles spanning subjects from Artificial Intelligence to Women's Studies, *The Basics* are an ideal starting point for students seeking to understand a subject area.

Each text comes with recommendations for further study and gradually introduces the complexities and nuances within a subject.

PRAGMATICS
BILLY CLARK

SEMIOTICS (FOURTH EDITION)
DANIEL CHANDLER

ENGLISH VOCABULARY
MICHAEL McCARTHY

TRANSLATION (SECOND EDITION)
JULIANE HOUSE

MEDIEVAL LITERATURE
ANGELA JANE WEISL AND ANTHONY JOSEPH CUNDER

ELT
MICHAEL McCARTHY AND STEVE WALSH

For a full list of titles in this series, please visit www.routledge.com/The-Basics/book-series/B

ELT

THE BASICS

Michael McCarthy and Steve Walsh

Routledge
Taylor & Francis Group

LONDON AND NEW YORK

Designed cover image: © Getty Images | DrAfter123

First published 2024
by Routledge
4 Park Square, Milton Park, Abingdon, Oxon OX14 4RN

and by Routledge
605 Third Avenue, New York, NY 10158

Routledge is an imprint of the Taylor & Francis Group, an informa business

© 2024 Michael McCarthy and Steve Walsh

British Library Cataloguing-in-Publication Data
A catalogue record for this book is available from the British Library

Library of Congress Cataloging-in-Publication Data
Names: McCarthy, Michael, 1947– author. | Walsh, Steve, 1959– author.
Title: ELT : the basics / Michael McCarthy and Steve Walsh.
Other titles: English language teaching
Description: Abingdon, Oxon ; New York, NY : Routledge, 2023. | Series: The basics |
    Includes bibliographical references and index.
Identifiers: LCCN 2023018520 (print) | LCCN 2023018521 (ebook) |
    ISBN 9781032395616 (hardback) | ISBN 9781032395609 (paperback) |
    ISBN 9781003350316 (ebook)
Subjects: LCSH: English language—Study and teaching.
Classification: LCC PE1065 .M3726 2023 (print) | LCC PE1065 (ebook) |
    DDC 428.0071—dc23/eng/20230802
LC record available at https://lccn.loc.gov/2023018520
LC ebook record available at https://lccn.loc.gov/2023018521

ISBN: 978-1-032-39561-6 (hbk)
ISBN: 978-1-032-39560-9 (pbk)
ISBN: 978-1-003-35031-6 (ebk)

DOI: 10.4324/9781003350316

Typeset in Bembo
by Apex CoVantage, LLC

To the memory of Ron Carter, friend and fellow traveller

CONTENTS

ACKNOWLEDGEMENTS

Elena (real name withheld), for permission to reproduce the compositions on pages 53, 54, and 61.

Áine Walsh, for permission to reproduce the images on pages 23, 28, 37, 42, 97, 99, 106, 111, 123, 126, 130, 139, 146, 150, 156, and 177.

Carmen Muñoz and the *Talkbank* project, for permission to reproduce the transcript on page 55.

Paul Miller and Jon Haines, for permission to reproduce the image on page 161.

The Cambridge University ALTA team, for permission to reproduce the transcript on page 176.

The teachers (names anonymised) who agreed to be interviewed (pages 109, 143, and 144).

INTRODUCTION TO THE READER

ENGLISH LANGUAGE TEACHING (ELT) BASICS

The basics of ELT can be boiled down to a handful of questions: WHAT? WHO? WHY? WHEN? WHERE? and HOW?

- WHAT do we teach? Simple answer: the English language. But there is a lot to say about what seems a simple answer, and that is where we start in this book.
- WHO is involved? We need to know as much as possible about our students to do the job properly. We also need to know what best practice is for a teacher. What does it mean to be a successful ELT teacher?
- WHY? Different students have different reasons, motivations, and goals for learning English. And you may have different reasons and goals for being a teacher.
- WHEN? A long course of two or three years spread over a number of school/academic terms, possibly with some school subjects being taught through English medium, is quite different from an intensive pre-university course for learners of academic English. Primary school learners have different needs from those learning in retirement.
- WHERE? The most common answer would be 'in a classroom'. The more we know about classrooms, how they work, and what goes on in them, the better. But the physical classroom is not the only place where people learn; online is another 'where', as is learning outside of institutions.

• HOW? There is no one correct or best way to teach English, though, based on our years of experience, knowledge of the profession, and familiarity with relevant research, we try to guide you to the most appropriate methods and resources for different teaching situations.

Each of these questions could generate a whole book, so in the limited space of this one, we will stick to the essentials. Once you have covered the basics, there is plenty more reading and research available – enough to last a lifetime.

THE RAW MATERIAL
LANGUAGE KNOWLEDGE

THE *EL* IN ELT

This book is about English language teaching. The English language is the raw material we utilise to impart knowledge of the language and the skills involved in using it. However, the term *the English language* is not as simple and straightforward as it may seem at first glance. It combines two surprisingly complex notions: *language* and *English*.

Language enables us to communicate. For most people, this means speaking and writing, using words. We can also use our bodies and facial expressions to make signs (especially where speaking or hearing is not possible), and we have mathematical symbols to express complex scientific notions, but all types of language exist for communication (Figure 1.1).

Three key features of human language enable communication: **substance**, **form**, and **meaning**. All human languages possess these, and all three are involved in English language teaching.

SUBSTANCE

THE STUFF OF LANGUAGE

Substance means the media through which we communicate. There are two types: phonic and graphic. **Phonic substance** is sound; we use our vocal apparatus to produce sounds which, when combined in certain ways, create meaning. The sounds leave our mouth and are received by the ears of the person(s) we address, what Peter

DOI: 10.4324/9781003350316-1

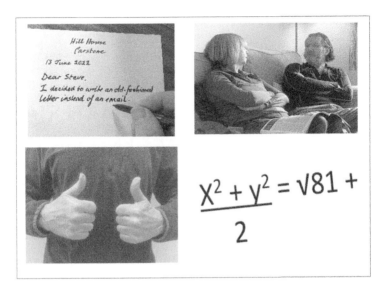

Figure 1.1 Types of language.
Source: Images © M. J. McCarthy 2023.

Roach calls 'the speech chain' (2001: 3–5). The study of sounds is **phonetics**.

The other type of substance is **graphic substance**; we use sets of letters or other types of symbols to communicate through writing. Speaking is the more basic and most frequent human activity – all languages have a spoken form, but not all have ever been written down. However, as Gerald Knowles points out, a large number of words we know come to us when we encounter them in reading, so the relationship between the phonic substance and the graphic substance is not a simple dividing line (Knowles 2014: 6–7).

SOUNDS

The phonic substance of English consists of sets of sounds which English speakers of different varieties agree on over time as belonging to their language. The study of how these sounds form a system is **phonology**. The English set of sounds may overlap with other languages, but there are often notable differences.

Each language has an agreed-upon set of sounds which are the basis of meaningful communication. These sets of sounds are called **phonemes**. Because they are sounds, and because the same letter of the alphabet can represent different sounds in English, we represent phonemes using **phonemic symbols**, not letters. You will often find these listed in dictionaries and alongside each word to tell you how it is normally pronounced. Table 1.1 shows a selection of English phonemes, with phonemic symbols and examples of words which contain them.

The phonemes in Table 1.1 fall into two groups: the left-hand column are **consonants**; the right-hand column are **vowels**. Consonants are made by momentarily stopping the air from flowing in some way, for example, by closing your lips (e.g., p, b, as in *pot or big*). Vowels are made by not blocking the air with your lips or teeth or tongue (e.g., e, ɒ, as in *met, lot*).

English has **consonant clusters** (consonants which immediately follow one another with no vowels in between), which can be difficult for non-English speakers, for example, *three, crisps, months, strain*. Some languages don't like to start words with certain combinations of consonants: Spanish, for example, doesn't like to start words with *s* + consonant and uses an *e*-vowel to begin with, so in Spanish, *Spain* is *España*, and *school is escuela*.

We can use our tongue to slide quickly from one vowel to another to produce a **diphthong**, which sounds like a single sound. Table 1.2 shows examples of diphthongs.

Table 1.1 Examples of English phonemes.

Phoneme	Example words	Phoneme	Example words
p	*party, cap*	iː	*mean, feet*
k	*case, black*	e	*get, head*
b	*brown, probe*	ɒ	*hot, what*
f	*fine, free*	æ	*cat, back*
tʃ	*cheese, much*	ʌ	*but, fun*
dʒ	*jump, badge*	uː	*boot, who*

Table 1.2 Examples of English diphthongs.

Diphthong	Example words
əʊ	*home, coat*
aʊ	*house, now*
aɪ	*ride, like*

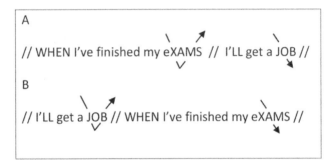

Figure 1.2 Discourse intonation choices.

INTONATION

Contrary to some traditional views, **intonation**, the movement of the voice up and down, is not so much concerned with either grammar or emotions but with interaction, the central theme of this book. David Brazil's (1997) description of intonation shows how the choice of rising and falling tones reflects the speaker's assumptions about the degree of shared or background knowledge (involving **referring** tones) as opposed to new information (using **proclaiming** tones). This choice is represented in two possible versions of the sentence in Figure 1.2.

The syllables in capitals in Figure 1.2 are stressed. In version A, *exams* has a fall-rise tone, meaning 'context/background to the statement'. *Job* is proclaimed – it is the new/main information. In version B, the listener may have said *Why don't you get a job?* The speaker effectively says, 'I will, but not till I've finished my exams' – *exams* is now new/proclaimed, while *job* is shared (referred).

WRITING

In the case of English, writing involves the use of a 26-letter alphabet; punctuation; spaces; and conventions such as headings, paragraphs, underlining, italics, and boldface, all of which communicate meaning visually, and we typically write horizontally, from left to right, though for special effect we might write vertically, from top to bottom. Other languages may do things differently. Chinese languages have a variety of ways of writing, sometimes using pictographs (pictorial symbols), sometimes using ideographs (symbols representing the idea of something). Some languages write from right to left (Arabic); others write traditionally from top to bottom (Korean, Japanese). No writing system is inferior or less logical in comparison with the widely used Roman alphabet of English.

Beginning learners of English as a second or foreign language may have already had exposure to the English alphabet owing to the global domination of English in many areas of life. Nonetheless, for a beginner, an encounter with a new writing system is likely to make learning English a greater mountain to climb than for a student coming from a language that already uses the same alphabet as English.

PERSONAL REFLECTION

Look at this back-to-front English sentence and consider how difficult it might be to adapt to a different orientation of written language.

.GNIDAER NEHW NOITCERID EGNAHC OT YSAE TON S'TI

One of the biggest challenges in English writing is spelling. Before the invention of printing, there were no hard and fast rules about how to spell English words. Printing helped to standardise spelling, but present-day spelling often represents earlier pronunciations – English spelling got historically 'stuck' (McCarthy 2023: 48). Spellings such as *knee* and *knob*, with their silent *k*, are leftovers of an earlier stage when the *k* was pronounced. Perfetti and Harris (2017), although writing with native-speaker (L1) learners in mind, show just how tricky learning to read in English can be because of spelling oddities.

Spellings may vary between British English (BrE) and North American English (AmE): *color* and *favor* (AmE) are *colour* and *favour* in BrE. *Center* and *theater* (AmE) are *centre* and *theatre* in BrE. Even knowing where to write a space between words is not entirely straightforward. We might write *She is well known* with a space between *well* and *known*, and we might be inclined to write *a well-known architect* with a hyphen, but English speakers would not typically write *a wellknown architect* (for more examples, see McCarthy 2023: 10–11).

FORM

WORDS

Substance is not just sounds or letters thrown together in any old fashion. Consonants and vowels combine to form syllables, and syllables combine to form words. Words are meaningful units of language. All the words of English together form the vocabulary, another term for which is **lexis**.

INFORMATION ADD-ON

The number of syllables in an English word can vary from one to more than a dozen for some specialised scientific words. Most everyday words have far fewer syllables. Here are some examples.

one syllable (monosyllabic)	*tree, look*
two syllables (disyllabic)	*paper, diesel*
three syllables (trisyllabic)	*competence, internet*
four syllables	*continental, operator*
five syllables	*examination, unfortunately*
six syllables	*reinterpretation, archaeological*
seven syllables	*compartmentalisation, extraterritorial*

The more syllables a word has, the more specialised and complex its meaning tends to be.

Words have phonic and graphic substance, and they have form. We know when we are in the presence of an English word, just as we know when we see or hear something that is not an English word. We know that *glass* is an English word, but *ssalg* is not – we might suspect *ssalg* could be a word from an exotic language we know nothing about, but we know it is not an English word. Neither the spelling nor the pronunciation follows the normal conventions of English words, and the sounds and letters don't mean anything.

A word must contain at least one bit of language that *means* something to the speakers of that language. The word *egg* has one syllable, and that syllable means something in English. The word *singer* has two syllables: a syllable meaning an action (*sing*), and one meaning 'person who does something' (*er*). The word *lettuce* has two syllables but only one element that means something, in this case, the whole word. The elements which mean something are called **morphemes**. We can define a word as an item consisting of at least one morpheme.

English words build and combine in various ways to produce new or more complex meanings. We add prefixes and suffixes, as in **re**write (prefix in bold) and *beauti**ful*** (suffix in bold). The prefixed and suffixed versions are **derived words**. Words combine to form **compounds**, where two or more words create a fixed form that has a single meaning, as in *car park*, *lampshade* and *electric car charger*. Making compounds and derived words are the two most important ways in which we introduce new words into English. McCarthy (2023: ch. 1) gives examples of other ways in which new words are created.

Words often combine in sequences of anything from two to five or six words which occur time and time again, many of which occur so frequently that they become verbal routines, often referred to as **chunks** or **clusters**, **lexical bundles**, or **formulaic sequences** (Schmitt 2004: 3–4). In this book we will use the familiar term *chunks* (see examples in Table 1.3). Chunks occur in writing and speaking but are particularly common in everyday conversation. This is because conversation happens in real time; we need to be able to retrieve chunks automatically and immediately without stopping for planning time. If we had to retrieve every word one by one, we could never speak fluently.

Table 1.3 Examples of everyday chunks.

Two-word chunks	Three-word chunks	Four-word chunks
you know	I think so	at the same time
I mean	at the moment	in the middle of
thank you	if you like	and things like that
good morning	by the way	as a result of

The chunks in Table 1.3 are common, everyday ones that are relatively easy to understand. Some seem complete in themselves (*good morning, at the moment*); others need something else to make complete sense (*in the middle of . . ., as a result of . . .*). Sometimes, chunks will have meanings that are not clear from the words that compose them: these are **idioms**. Examples of common idioms include *get rid of, chill out, be over the moon, out of the blue*.

GRAMMAR

English words are subject to conventions that govern their grammatical behaviour. **Grammar** is the set of conventions that govern how we put together phrases, clauses, and (in writing) sentences. In this book we talk of *conventions* rather than *rules*. **Conventions** are social agreements as to how things operate, and they can and do change over time. However, most people think of grammar as rules, a bit like rules and laws handed down by authorities that we must obey, and that grammar rules dictate what is correct and incorrect.

Traditionally, grammars did indeed provide rules or prescriptions, rather as a doctor gives a patient a prescription, a set of actions which must be followed to the letter. Such grammars were **prescriptive** grammars which listed rules for how the language should be used correctly. 'Rules' can be very useful; for example, it is useful to know that, in standard educated English, verbs need an -*s* ending in the third person singular present tense: we say *(s)he/it works , arrives* , and so on. This does not mean that dialect speakers in certain parts of eastern England who say *(s)he/it work, arrive* are 'wrong', are 'breaking the rules', or are speaking 'bad English'; the conventions of their dialect grammar are simply different from those of standard English. Stating what the conventions are, based on the evidence of actual use, is **descriptive** grammar. Descriptive grammar makes no value judgement of good or bad English; it simply describes what is normally the case. Grammar becomes more like what happens *as a rule* rather than *the rules*. Nonetheless, as Elizabeth Peterson points out, public attitudes towards grammar can be quite prescriptive, and the uneducated, the young, and other marginalised social groups are often condemned for their grammar (Peterson 2020). Notions of 'good' and 'bad' English are deeply rooted in people's minds.

To describe the grammar of English, we need categories for how certain patterns repeat themselves time and time again, so, for example, in describing phrases, we can observe patterns resulting from the grammatical conventions in operation in present-day English. Table 1.4 has examples of different types of phrases.

In Table 1.4, we see how phrases are often part of larger patterns which are **clauses**. Clauses contain a verb phrase and often have noun phrases and other phrases attached, for example, *it **arrives** at 10.30, the printer **isn't** **working**, I'm quite tired, we **drove** slowly*.

These patterns are called **structures** because they build meanings by relating words and phrases to one another in different ways: sometimes there's a subject, a 'doer'; sometimes there's an object (the person or thing 'done to'); sometimes there's an adverbial

Table 1.4 Examples of types of English phrases.

Type	Pattern	Examples
Noun phrase	Group of words with a noun as the **head** (i.e., the central, most important word)	*music, the big **house**, that **shop** on the corner*
Verb phrase	Group with a verb as the head	*it **arrives** at 10.30, the printer isn't **working***
Adjective phrase	Group with an adjective as the head	*it's a **nice** house, I'm quite **tired***
Adverb phrase	Group with an adverb as the head	*we drove **slowly**, he is **highly** educated*
Prepositional phrase	Group with a preposition plus a noun phrase	*we're **at** the beach, come **in** the morning*

phrase telling us where, when, how, and so on (e.g., *at 10.30, suddenly*). The system of how we organise structures into sentences is called **syntax**. English sentences generally stick to the pattern subject-verb-object when making statements, as do Scandinavian languages. Spanish has more flexibility and does not always need to state the subject. English is often classified as an SVO language (subject-verb-object); other languages may use SOV (e.g., Korean), VSO (e.g., Filipino), or other sequences.

So far, we've treated vocabulary (lexis) and grammar as though they were two streams which run parallel. This is not a true picture of how grammar and lexis interact, and, although language teaching syllabuses and lesson timetables often separate them, there is good reason to consider them together, under the heading of what is called **lexicogrammar**.

One way of describing how lexis and grammar interact is **pattern grammar**. In pattern grammar what is important are the different patterns that typically surround a word Hunston and Francis 2000). Finding such patterns efficiently and quickly is made easier by having a **corpus**. A corpus (plural **corpora**) is a computerised collection of texts which can be analysed using dedicated software to count how often or how rarely something occurs in the texts. Consider, for example, the word *certain* and how it occurs in the more than 4,000 written and spoken texts in the 100-million-word 1994 British National Corpus (BNC).[1] These are some of the repeated patterns we find:

1. *Almost certain* occurs 321 times. The most common verb used with it is *be*, as in *I'm almost certain*.
2. Of the examples with *be*, 43 occur as *almost certain to be*, and 22 of these are *is almost certain to be*.
3. *A certain* occurs more than 5,000 times and is typically followed by a noun (e.g., *a certain sequence, a certain amount*).
4. *A certain* occurs 225 times in the pattern *to a certain extent*.

The patterns with *almost certain* seem to mean 'almost 100% sure' (sense A), while the patterns with *a certain* indicate 'a specific/

particular amount/extent' (sense B). So, we have two different senses of the word *certain*: sense A is seen in 1 and 2; sense B is seen in 3 and 4. Each sense is associated with particular syntactic patterns.

Another way of understanding lexicogrammar is slightly different but also shows how grammar and lexis interact with each other. This approach is associated with **systemic functional grammar**, where all the elements of the language are seen as fitting together in systems that present language users with choices, such as *present* versus *past* in the tense system but, equally, choices in the systems of lexis, such as choosing verbs expressing actions versus verbs expressing events or mental processes. Each choice creates patterns where the lexical choices interact with the grammatical conventions. This approach is associated with the grammatical theories of Michael Halliday and is often referred to as the Hallidayan approach. Halliday's major work is his *Introduction to Functional Grammar*, where the notion of lexicogrammar is fully elaborated upon (2014).

MEANING

HEALTH, SAFETY, AND DINOSAURS

The substance and form of language together communicate meanings. The study of meaning is called **semantics**. The forms – the lexical forms of words and chunks, and the grammatical forms of grammar words and structures/patterns, have meanings which emerge from the lexicogrammar.

We can examine the meaning of a word from two main viewpoints: (a) what the word means and (b) how the word relates to other words in the language. The former is concerned with the **denotation** of the word, its meaning in the world, the meaning you would expect to find in a dictionary. How the word relates to other words is called **sense relations**. Sense relations involve whether words are **synonyms** (e.g., *start* and *begin*) or **antonyms** (e.g., *start* and *finish*), whether they belong to a **lexical set** (e.g., *blue, yellow, green, red*, etc.), or whether they are **hyponyms**; for example *rose, tulip, daffodil* are all hyponyms of the **superordinate** *flower*. For more on denotation and sense relations, see the book on vocabulary in this series (McCarthy 2023).

As well as denotations, words can have **connotations**, feelings or ideas associated with them through experiencing them in particular contexts. For instance, the words *health* and *safety*, taken individually, have positive connotations, but heard together, in the chunk *health and safety* (as in 'new health and safety regulations'), for many people, they have negative connotations of over-fussy, unnecessary, and exaggerated regulations.

The denotation of a word is often referred to as its literal meaning, but words can also be used **figuratively**, with a meaning that extends the literal meaning into an unusual or creative context. A *dinosaur* is the name for a kind of long-extinct animal species; it can also be used figuratively, as a **metaphor** to refer to someone or something that is resistant to change when the world around it has changed. On metaphor generally, see Deignan (2005).

CORPUS EVIDENCE

The BNC 1994 has a number of occurrences of *dinosaur* which clearly exploit the figurative (metaphorical) meaning. Here are two examples. The symbol <s> means 'speaker'.

<s> Today the Opposition revealed themselves as dinosaurs because they acted as mere apologists for the old established order. (BNC1994 HHW)

<s> . . . these industries are dinosaurs, they're using technology that's thirty years out of date. (BNC1994 HYL)

WHAT DO *YOU* MEAN?

Semantics is the study of meaning. We attempt to answer the question, 'What does this word/expression mean?' But there is another question we can ask: 'What does the *speaker* mean by using a particular word or expression in this context?' The study of meaning in context is called **pragmatics** (see O'Keeffe et al. 2020 for an introduction). Pragmatics deals with speakers' meanings and intentions. If someone says, 'Gosh! It's already eleven o'clock!', they might be making an excuse to get away from a boring social encounter. What matters is not the direct meaning of the words in the world; what matters is what the speaker hopes to achieve by using those words, that is to say, the **illocutionary force** of the utterance.

Pragmatics is more concerned with what people *do* with language rather than just the words they use. The speaker who says, 'Can you turn the volume down?' might be genuinely enquiring whether a piece of equipment has a volume control or, depending on the relationship between speaker and listener, a command to lower the volume (an example of a *directive*). Actions such as enquiring, making requests, or issuing directives are **speech acts**. Other examples of speech acts are apologising, complimenting, thanking, congratulating, and so on. Speech acts form the basis of the **communicative approach** in language teaching, where 'doing' with language and achieving communicative goals is the central focus (see Chapter 4).

COMPLETING THE LANGUAGE PUZZLE

THE DISCOURSE PROCESS

We have considered the sorts of patterns that emerge when grammar and vocabulary interact in lexicogrammar. Putting lexis and grammar together is rather like connecting the pieces of a jigsaw puzzle, and a jigsaw puzzle might be a good metaphor for language (Figure 1.3). The multitude of pieces, those which will fit together and those which will not, when appropriately assembled, create one harmonious and meaningful picture. The activity of producing meaningful 'pictures' (in the case of language, meaningful *texts*) is **discourse**. Looking at discourse instead of just looking at the individual language 'pieces' (e.g., words, phrases, sentences) gives us a birds-eye view of something bigger, something 'beyond the sentence', where language is put to work to create meanings in context (McCarthy and Clancy 2019). In the world of discourse, we are dealing with texts and their contexts.

Texts can be written texts such as newspaper articles, blogs, novels, language course books, and academic essays or spoken texts such as conversations, podcasts, lectures, emails, news broadcasts, and so on. Texts grow out of interaction among participants (e.g., friends chatting, teachers and students talking in class, students

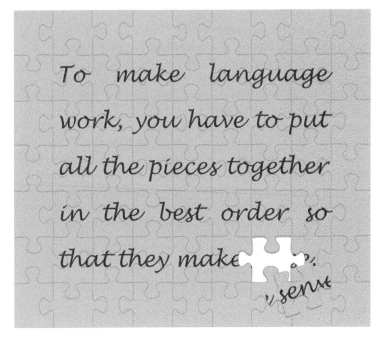

Figure 1.3 The language jigsaw puzzle.
Source: Image © the authors 2022.

writing essays for their tutors, journalists writing articles for their readers). The participants all have roles in the process. You might be a student in class; out of class you might be an employee reporting to your superior. Each role will vest in you rights and responsibilities in the discourse process. As a student, you probably have no right to take control of the lesson and to decide who speaks when; as a teacher, you have the responsibility to make sure the lesson does not collapse into 50 minutes of embarrassing silence.

Brian Paltridge's introduction to the study of discourse stresses the relationship between texts and their contexts (2022: ch.1). If we take a discourse-based approach to ELT, we focus not just on the conventions of grammar and how they may be correctly used, or just the denotation or the pronunciation of words, but also what is appropriate at the discourse level. This will include making choices about formality and informality, of general or special vocabulary, of use or non-use of highly idiomatic expressions, exploiting the grammar and lexis (or the phonology in speech) to create coherence, dividing a text into paragraphs, and so on. In speaking it will mean who speaks when (turn-taking), how people start and end conversations, how teachers manage their lessons and interact with their students. In writing it will mean structuring a piece of writing so that it is clear for the reader, who is usually not present at the time or in the place that the text is produced.

DISCOURSE IN THE CLASSROOM

Think back to your schooldays. If they were like ours, you will have memories of the teacher doing a lot of talking, asking questions, imparting knowledge to you, testing you on that knowledge, praising you, giving you a telling-off for not working hard enough or being late, and so on. You probably only spoke when spoken to, when you were allowed to do some sort of task with other students, or when you put your hand up to ask the teacher something. Your role in the discourse of the classroom was definitely a secondary one; the primary role and rights of speaking belonged to the teacher. Consider this simple, invented example:

Teacher: What is the capital of Japan?
Student: Tokyo.
Teacher: Tokyo. Yes, Tokyo. Well done.

The teacher initiates the interaction by asking a question. The student responds, then the teacher follows up by acknowledging the response and affirming that it's the desired answer. We can now label these three lines. Together they make up an **exchange**.

   I = initiation, R = response, F = follow-up

I   Teacher: What is the capital of Japan?
R   Student: Tokyo.
F   Teacher: Tokyo. Yes, Tokyo. Well done.

This type of exchange happens many times in classrooms, not only language classrooms. Let's now add a complication:

I   Teacher: What is the capital of Japan?
R   Student 1: Seoul?
F1   Teacher: [silence]
R2   Student 2: Tokyo?
F2   Teacher: Tokyo. Yes, Tokyo. Well done.

Students know instinctively that if the teacher withholds a response, then the answer is probably wrong, so another student (Student 2) has a go and gets it right. The teacher affirms that it is the right answer. Looping back and forth between response and follow-up can continue until someone gets the right answer or else the teacher steps in and provides the answer. And it goes without saying that here the teacher knew the answer all along. Questions like these are called **display questions**; their purpose is to put knowledge 'on display' for the whole class. They are not the sort of question we normally ask people in everyday conversation when we want to know something unless we genuinely don't know the answer or are laying a verbal trap for them.

I, R, and F together are often referred to as **the IRF pattern**. Here we have given a simplified picture of it. In Chapter 6 we will take things further. IRF is at the heart of the classroom discourse process.

RESEARCH EVIDENCE

In the 1970s, John Sinclair and Malcom Coulthard recorded mother-tongue primary school classes in England. Based on the lesson transcripts, they devised the IRF system to describe exchanges between teachers and pupils. They noted that it was teachers who initiated and controlled the exchanges and that exchanges linked together to form longer transactions that represented phases of the lesson. They also broke the exchanges down into various smaller speech acts. Their work (Sinclair and Coulthard 1975) remains one of the first and most important developments in what became known as **discourse analysis**.

TEMPLATES AND GENRES

Good written texts are coherent and are written in a way that makes the writer's meaning clear and makes life as easy as possible for the reader. Over the years, we read hundreds of texts and come to expect that they will take a particular form appropriate to their context and purpose and to the writer-reader relationship. Just as repeated use of grammatical forms creates and reinforces the grammatical conventions, discourse conventions emerge from repeated patterns of use in written texts. These patterns become **rhetorical templates** which writers use to structure their texts in order to build arguments to persuade their readers.

Michael Hoey showed how certain patterns were very common, for example, the **problem-solution** pattern. Many thousands of texts are about problems and possible solutions, and student essays are often based on describing a problem and offering solutions. We can represent the problem-solution template in the form of a flow-chart (Figure 1.4).

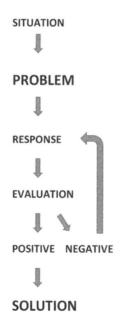

Figure 1.4 The problem-solution template (based on Hoey 2001).

Problem-solution texts start with describing a situation and establishing the context. Then comes a statement of the problem – simply describing the context is not enough; we need to know what the problem is. Then the writer offers a possible response or responses. Each possible response is evaluated. If the evaluation is positive – the proposed solution will (probably) work – then the text can wrap up and finish. If the evaluation is negative – the response is inadequate or will clearly not work – then the text can loop back to evaluate other responses, until the writer is satisfied that the response will have a positive outcome. The problem-solution text is not the only template, but it is an extremely common one. Further text types are explored in Hoey's (2001) introduction to written discourse analysis.

Another way of looking at the discourse process is to consider how typical written texts emerge from particular contexts, for example, academic texts. You are probably familiar with what an academic article looks like, and if you follow up the references in this book, you will encounter many more. An academic article may well follow the problem-solution rhetorical template or another (such as articles which investigate and evaluate theoretical claims), but whichever template it uses, you will expect it to follow certain conventions. There will be a title, usually an abstract, and a report of work already accomplished in the field; significant works will be cited; the style will be formal and the content will be highly focused upon the subject at hand, with evidence presented, such as tables, diagrams or other visuals; and there will be some sort of conclusion at the end. The academic article has evolved as a **genre** over the centuries, just as novels and short stories, student dissertations, or newspaper editorials have. Becoming familiar with and practising genres is important for students learning English for professional or academic purposes, where writing essays, reports, reviews, sales pitches, advertisements, and so on may be involved.

WRITING, SPEAKING, OR BOTH AT ONCE?

There is more to say about the relationship between speaking and writing than the fact that one uses sound and the other visual symbols. In the discourse process, the two ways of communicating result in different types of texts. Academic articles and novels, for instance, are written to be read typically at a different place and time from the time and place of their creation. Informal, everyday face-to-face conversations happen in real time; they are created and received simultaneously. These differences are often manifested in the frequency lists that are produced when we compare spoken and written corpora. Although there is a great deal of overlap between spoken and written language, some of the variation in frequency lists tells us a lot about the differences in the discourse process between speaking and writing.

One example is the distribution of sentence connectors. Sentence connectors link ideas and include items such as *therefore, thus, consequently, subsequently, furthermore, nevertheless*. All these words are available to anyone using English, but conventions have evolved so that they have become associated with particular types of discourse, especially more formal ones. These can include spoken discourses such as academic lectures, formal speeches, debates, and so on, where, just as in writing, it is important to signal to the receiver how the speech works logically and coherently. Nonetheless, if we compare two large corpora of informal speaking and formal writing, we see that our example sentence connectors show a definite bias towards formal writing; they seem to have become a 'fingerprint' of formal written discourses. Figure 1.5 shows the difference

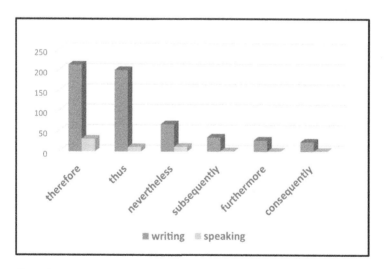

Figure 1.5 Sentence connectors: writing and speaking.

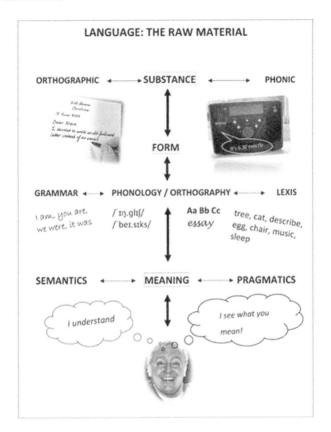

Figure 1.6 Substance, form, and meaning.
Source: Image © the authors 2023.

in their frequency in the written texts of the BNC 1994 and the transcripts of the Spoken BNC of 2014. The graph shows occurrences per million words.

Writers of materials for ELT often take such statistical information into account, especially in designing materials for specific groups of learners such as those on business English or academic English courses.

It is an over-simplification to look at speaking and writing as two activities separate and distinct from each other. Some texts are written but are meant to be spoken, for example, scripted radio and TV broadcasts, and nowadays, many examples of discourse that are 'written' (insomuch as they are typed on a keyboard) display all the characteristics of conversation. The back-and-forth of online chat, text messaging and rapid exchanges of email often resemble the turn taking of face-to-face conversation. The traditional dividing lines between speaking and writing have become blurred in the presence of blogs, SMS texts, and social media posts. All this is as much part of the *WHAT?* of ELT as the reading passages, essay-writing, and oral practice many of us will recall from our experience of learning a foreign language.

So far in this chapter we have looked at the basics of language within a three-part framework of substance, form, and meaning. We sum this up in Figure 1.6.

By the time we get to the bottom of Figure 1.6, we see that language is all about exchanging meaning, and doing so in contexts, with other people. In other words, language is all about **interaction**. Interaction will be at the heart of all our discussions in this book, whatever aspects of ELT we are considering. In the next sections, we look at what 'English' in the phrase *English language* means in the world today.

ENGLISH IN THE WORLD

FROM VARIATION TO VARIETIES

The previous section touched on the way different types of discourse evolve from their contexts of use, and the discussion centred around speaking and writing and special cases of language use such as classroom language, academic discourse, and online communication. But language also varies as a result of other factors. For example, teenagers typically have their own style of speaking, with its own pronunciation and vocabulary, which enables them to identify with their peers and age group. 'Teenage English' is an example of a **sociolect**, as reflected in the COLT corpus (Corpus of London Teenage language; Stenström et al. 2002). Age, gender, ethnicity, culture, and social class can all influence people's speaking style. Having a broad view of socially determined variation in English offers the potential for enriching learners' exposure to and experience of the language.

RESEARCH EVIDENCE

Australian English is one of the independent varieties of English that have grown up over the last couple of centuries. It has its own distinctive pronunciation and vocabulary. One feature of its vocabulary is a fondness for clipping words (making them shorter), for example, *football* becomes *footie*, and *afternoon* becomes *arvo*. There is evidence that younger generations have adopted clippings of technical terms, such as *lappy* for *laptop*. In this way, we can see both a dialect and a sociolect in action.

Research has also focused on the way Australian adolescents quote speech (e.g., using *be like*, and *go*) in narratives and reports (Winter 2002).

For more examples of Australian English, see the article '7 Bonzer Aussie Words' on the *Merriam-Webster Dictionary* website at www.merriam-webster.com/words-at-play/7-bonzer-australian-words. See also the *Australian Geographic* website at www.australiangeographic.com.au/news/2010/08/why-we-shorten-barbie-footy-and-arvo/.

ACCENTS AND DIALECTS

We often hear people say things like, 'She has a foreign accent' or 'He sounds foreign'. What we perceive in someone's **accent** is different pronunciation and perhaps a different rhythm or general voice setting that makes someone sound different from us or different from the prevailing standard in whatever part of the English-speaking world we find ourselves. Everyone has an accent – it may be a standard, educated accent; it may be an accent associated with a particular sociolect; or it may be associated with a particular county, region, or national language. In the case of a 'foreign' accent, a non-native user's pronunciation is typically influenced by the phonology of their first language. But the characteristic pronunciations of the different varieties of English around the world are also often influenced by **language contact**, when communities speaking different tongues mix, trade, and do business, colonise, and so on. Thus, the varieties of English spoken in Wales and Ireland have been influenced by contact with the Celtic languages of those two countries for centuries. Further afield, trade and colonisation resulted in contact between South Asian and East Asian languages and English, giving us the distinctive English accents of countries such as India, Malaysia, and Singapore.

The widely differing countries where English is used as a main or official language have also developed their own grammar and vocabulary. Taken all together, the combinations of different accent, grammar and vocabulary in different given geographical regions gives us **dialects** (Crystal 2018). Even a small country like the United Kingdom has different dialects; for example, in the counties of Yorkshire or Norfolk, dialectal differences can be heard. Across the English-speaking world, there are many dialects of English which are widely separated geographically, from the Caribbean to South and East Asia, to Africa and the Pacific region, all of which have an equal claim to be established varieties of English alongside the more globally dominant varieties such as standard, educated British, or North American English. The current global situation of English means we can speak in the plural of 'Englishes', and the term **World Englishes** has become widely accepted to describe the different national and regional varieties of English (see Schneider 2020). Figure 1.7 shows a simplified map indicating world regions where English has become an official and/or widely used language in daily life.

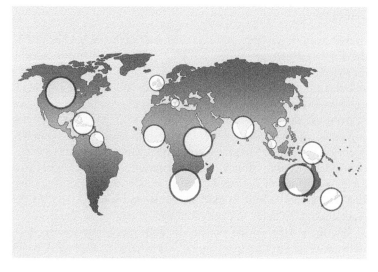

Figure 1.7 English around the world.
Source: Image © Áine Walsh 2023.

Another aspect of variation in the use of English, one that is increasingly important as globalisation has evolved, is when people use English as a language in common, even though none of them may have English as their first language. This often happens in international business contexts (Nickerson 2005). For example, a Swedish exporter might use English to do deals with a Korean customer, with both sides having a sufficient command of English to communicate successfully. This is the use of English as a **lingua franca**. At any given moment, millions of people around the world use English in this way. *Lingua franca* English cannot be said to be an established dialect, as its grammar and vocabulary will shift and vary for every different circumstance, and it is not associated with any particular accent. It will reflect the users' geographical, social, educational, and individual background, and speakers will often **accommodate** to their listeners; that is, they may simplify or reduce the range of their language to fit what they perceive to be the range of the listener's comprehension, and all parties will work hard at the pragmatic level to achieve their communicative goals (Kecskes 2019).

THEN WHAT?

In this chapter, we have outlined the basics of the *WHAT?* of ELT, the English language. Wherever you teach English in the world, knowledge of language and how it functions will be an indispensable feature of your claim to be an English language teacher. Having seen, even at this basic level, how sophisticated human language is, from the individual sounds and letters to the world of discourse and texts, and how the term 'the English language' hides complex historical, social, geographical and global issues, you will probably conclude that you will never know enough. That is certainly true for us as authors of this book, but there is a vast world of reading and information about English in books and journals and on the web, enough to keep you busy for years.

But then what? What do we do with this knowledge? Obviously, we share it with learners, but knowledge *about* English is not the same as skill in using it. Skills involve the application of knowledge in real contexts. In the next chapter we look at the basic skills that form the foundation of ELT.

NOTE

1 See www.natcorp.ox.ac.uk/corpus/index.xml?ID=intro

FURTHER READING

McCarthy, M. J. 2021. *English Grammar: The Basics*. **Abingdon: Routledge**.
This book takes you through the basics of grammar, how English sentences are constructed, how some major theories of grammar have influenced description and teaching over the years, how English grammar has become the source of debate in education and public life, and the role of grammar in society,

McCarthy, M. J. 2023. *English Vocabulary: The Basics*. **Abingdon: Routledge**.
Here you will find the basics of English vocabulary, including how new words are formed, how English vocabulary evolved and changed over the centuries, how words are systematically related to one another, how children learn vocabulary, and the role of vocabulary in society.

Roach, P. 2001. *Phonetics*. **Oxford: Oxford University Press**.
This is a good, clear introduction to the study of basic speech sounds and how they combine to form vowels, consonants, and so on, building up to the complex systems of words, pronunciation, and intonation and continuous speech, and how factors such as regional variation, age, and social variation influence the phonology of a language.

O'Keeffe, A., Clancy, B. and Adolphs, S. 2020. *Introducing Pragmatics in Use*. **Second edition. Abingdon, Oxon: Routledge**.
This is an introduction to pragmatics by three well-known scholars in applied linguists. It shows how pragmatics is best seen in action when based on corpus evidence. It includes discussions and illustrations of topics such as politeness and speech acts and is written in a non-jargonistic, accessible style.

2

LANGUAGE SKILLS

KNOWLEDGE AND SKILL

Chapter 1 looked at the formal elements of English (phonology, grammar, lexis) and how they work together to create meanings and discourse. We also considered the term *English language* in light of today's global society. Knowledge of how English works and the status of English in the world are the most basic of ELT basics.

Now imagine. You get your students to read Chapter 1 of this book. They would gain knowledge *about* language. Next, you help them build their vocabulary, pronounce English intelligibly (in whatever variety you choose), and give them grammar charts showing how sentences are formed. This would be knowledge *of* language. All this could happen without the learners having an opportunity to use what they have learnt. You would be teaching **usage** rather than **use**.

Applying knowledge of language (*use*) involves **skills**. To engage in successful communication, we listen, speak, read, and write, using the resources of the language. Listening, speaking, reading, and writing are the **four skills** that have underpinned ELT for many decades. They are often divided into **receptive** skills (listening, reading) and **productive** skills (speaking, writing).

PERSONAL REFLECTION

The science of how a bicycle works involves pedals, gears, handlebars, brakes, and so on. But what skills are involved in efficient cycling?

DOI: 10.4324/9781003350316-2

THE COMMUNICATION MATRIX

For the authors of this book, a typical day can involve all the linguistic skills:

- We read a newspaper or news website or listen to the news on radio or TV.
- We write emails, text messages, and academic texts.
- We search for the latest research, read, and make notes.
- We sometimes silently prepare a talk, then may rehearse it out loud.
- We talk online to plan this book, decide who will write what, and write down what we agree.
- We engage in anecdotes, banter, and social chit-chat.
- We talk with others while doing domestic tasks such as cooking, cleaning, and shopping.
- We have face-to-face or online meetings with colleagues where an agenda is followed.
- We teach face-to-face and online via classes, lectures, seminars, and supervisions.
- We visit websites, read blogs, listen to podcasts, watch videos, shop online, and use social media.

The list involves all four skills, often more than one at a time. Some of them involve **output** such as speaking or writing; others are sources of **input** and may be received in silence. The four skills support one another; they are **integrated**. We read and talk about what we read (university students do this). We speak so that someone can write something down (e.g., telling someone our address); we write in order to remember things (a to-do list, a reminder). We listen and make notes (e.g., as audience members in a lecture). Interaction among the skills is not the exception; it is the norm. When we use the terms *receptive* and *productive*, it is a mistake to equate these with *passive* and *active*, respectively.

The skills operate in a matrix in where communication can flourish. The person in Figure 2.1 is attending a webinar and is reading what is on the screen, listening to the speaker, and writing notes, all at the same time. Each skill is interwoven with the others.

Figure 2.1 Webinar: interaction among skills.
Source: Image © Áine Walsh 2022.

In the case of a webinar, you can often choose to participate at the time it happens, or you can choose to watch a recorded version later, so your participation may be **synchronous** (happening at the same time) or **asynchronous** (happening at a different time); each will call upon different skills.

In engaging in communication, we do not just *act*; we **interact**. **Interaction** involves action between at least two participants (a reader and writer, a speaker and listener). Texts, written or spoken, are a third party in interaction; they are the vehicles that *mediate* between sender and recipient. The four skills are central to ELT because learning involves interaction, with a teacher, with class-mates, with teaching materials.

LISTENING

A STREAM OF SOUND

Hearing occurs constantly if we have normal hearing – wind, traffic, our footsteps, and so on. *Listening* means purposely attending to sound and making sense of it. When we listen to normally paced conversation, we do not process every morpheme or syllable in the same way. We take in the important words, which, in English, are the **stressed words**, words said with greater intensity and often given slightly longer duration than the 'background words' which scaffold the message. Stress may be given to unpredictable or 'surprising' words (Rühlemann and Schweinberger 2021). In this way, we give **prominence** to some words and make other words non-prominent. In this exchange, marked in capitals are words most likely to be prominent, with stressed syllables in bold:

Joe: D'you want **PAS**TA or **PIZZ**A?
Lisa: **PAS**TA if that's O**KAY**.
Joe: **RIGHT**.

When you hear a new language for the first time, all the sounds seem to merge into one another in a continuous stream; it is difficult to know where one word ends and another begins. This problem is got over by hearing words in more and more contexts and associating sounds with words already encountered in reading, so repetition is important, and reading and listening complement each other. However, learners may still have problems separating the stream of sound into meaningful words and expressions. This is a good argument for ways of teaching listening which prepare students better to be ready to encounter the speech stream. Throwing them in at the deep end with unedited, natural recordings can be very stressful.

INFORMATION ADD-ON

One of the authors of this book had a student who started an essay with the word *festival*, and, when queried, insisted it was something English speakers said when listing a sequence of points. He was mishearing *first of all* (McCarthy 2010a).

BEFORE, DURING AND AFTER

To avoid learners being overwhelmed by the speech stream, listening can be structured around *pre-listening*, *listening*, and *post-listening*. Pre-listening tasks activate topics in learners' minds before they listen to the target speech. They activate the learner's **schema** (plural **schemata**). Schemata are mental representations of phenomena, based on real word knowledge, cultural background, and experience. If we want students to listen to an airport announcement about a change of gate for a flight, we may start by talking about what happens at an airport when you fly and why it is important to listen to announcements. This prepares learners mentally to tackle the stream of speech in an airport announcement, by activating ideas and relevant vocabulary. Schemata facilitate **predicting** what might come next and **inferring** meaning where it is not directly stated or where the language is unfamiliar.

Sometimes individual words are the key to comprehension; other times, the appropriate schema enables the listener to infer meaning without understanding individual words. When comprehension of individual words is dominant, it is referred to as **bottom-up** listening; when the schema, prediction, and inferencing are dominant, it is a **top-down** process. Bottom-up and top-down processing may alternate or operate simultaneously – there is no rule as to which to use at any given moment. Applying one or the other in the most effective way, moment by moment, is an efficient strategy.

After listening, students can give feedback. What, if anything, was difficult (the speed, vocabulary, the speaker's accent, length of the listening passage, individual words, chunks)? That is one kind of 'after'; another is to see if the listening text generates further talk among the learners themselves, whether as pair-work, group-work, or a whole-class conversation. In this way, the listening text becomes a schema-activator for speaking.

TALKING BACK

Jack Richards says:

> In daily life, people are expected to understand what other people say, as well as to respond or react accordingly; they need to be able to do the hundred and one things that depend on listening.

(2015: 371)

'Respond or react accordingly' is central to all interaction. Response may take the form of sounds (*oh! uhuh*), body language (shrugging shoulders), words (*great, right*), or actions (e.g., following instructions). Listening lessons which try to reflect what happens in the world outside the classroom involve not just comprehending messages but also responding to them.

PERSONAL REFLECTION

If you were the hearer, how would you respond to these sentences? Words? Actions? Attention?

1   'Have you been teaching English long?'
2   'This is CNN news with the latest world headlines.'
3   'Your flight is now ready to board.'

We make a distinction between **listening comprehension** and **listen-and-respond**. Listen-and-respond activities provide a bridge between listening and speaking. Listeners are not passive recipients, nor do they only respond to incoming talk by nodding their head or saying *uhuh*, or *I understand*, or *yes* and *no*. Typically, they go further and show **good listenership** (McCarthy 2002). Good listenership is a core feature of everyday conversation. It is how we show our humanity and how we create and maintain social relations.

Using a corpus, McCarthy (2002) listed a set of lexical items which listeners exploit to feed back to speakers that (a) they have received the message, (b) they have understood it, and (c) they are *engaging* with it. The last point, (c), is where the listener shows empathy, emotion, agreement/disagreement, and other types of social involvement with the speaker before embarking on their own next contribution to the discourse. This includes words such as *right, wow, true, absolutely, great, sure, good*, and chunks with *that's* (*that's good/awful/too bad*, etc.). Most of these are vocabulary that learners acquire at an early stage, so listen-and-respond activities can give learners realistic practice without the extra burden of new vocabulary.

CORPUS EVIDENCE

This corpus extract shows some typical British English response items in bold. Other varieties of English may have different expressions for the same functions; for example, Anne O'Keeffe and Svenja Adolphs looked at Irish English responses (O'Keeffe and Adolphs 2008). Here <S1> and<S2> mean first and second speaker.

<S1> Er Jim across, across the road, is it Jim you play on a Thursday so . . .
<S2> **That's right**. Yes.
<S1> Yes, certainly give you his er . . .
<S2> **Right**.
<S1> phone number, yes.
<S2> **Thanks that's great**.
<S1> It's er I'll just, I'll just get my little book out and I'll tell you what it is.
<S2> **Right**.
<S1> It's er Darlington three four five six seven.
<S2> **Great that's smashing**.

(BNC 1994 JT5)

Good listenership is summed up in Figure 2.2, which traces the integration of listening and speaking.

Figure 2.2 illustrates that people show listenership by responding to what they've just heard before embarking on what they want to say, the **conversational increment**, which pushes the conversation forward.

BOX-TICKING

It may not be feasible in large classes to give everyone the opportunity to listen and respond, and listening activities are often designed simply to test learners' ability to comprehend spoken language. Teachers naturally want to find out whether learners understand what they hear, and sometimes it will be appropriate simply to test whether they have understood or got the wrong end of the stick

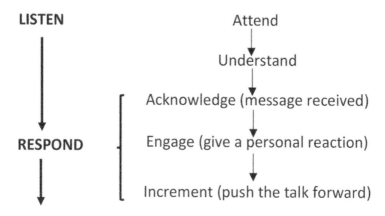

Figure 2.2 Good listenership.

(see Buck 2001: ch.1 for a full discussion). Testing is often done by multiple choice or box-ticking exercises as the learners listen.

THE TWO-SIDED COIN

The good listenership sequence (Figure 2.2) shows something basic about conversation: that, apart from the opening turn, all turns in a conversation are usually responses to what has gone before. As a consequence, the teaching of listening and speaking both have the teaching of responding at their heart. Speaking and listening become two sides of the same coin (McCarthy and McCarten 2023). Listen-and-respond activities can be personalised, giving students the chance to choose their own responses. The teacher may need to supply a repertoire of possible responses, but students can choose which ones best express their own reaction or can add their own (see McCarthy et al. 2014a: 71 for examples).

Michael Rost says: 'Listening is not only a skill area in language performance, but is also a critical means of acquiring a second language' (2001: 7). He also mentions other listening skills that are crucial for successful interaction, including recognising shifts to a new topic and strategies to repair communication problems. These are processes that happen regularly in language classrooms, where teachers generally have control over topics and learners have to keep their ears open to changes in the way the lesson is progressing and to the teacher's input alongside the lesson content.

Choosing listening material involves choosing whether to use dominant varieties such as North American English or to expose students to a range of accents and varieties of World Englishes. This decision may be taken out of your hands by the course book or the curriculum. But even in institutionally constrained contexts, it may still be possible to add extra listening materials to the syllabus. Rather than impose one model of English, it may be of benefit to expose learners to different varieties using online resources such as local radio stations from around the world or podcasts or online interviews with celebrities who use English as a lingua franca. As always, best practice involves respecting the constraints of the local context and the needs and goals of learners.

SPEAKING

GO WITH THE FLOW

To speak with a degree of fluency is one of the most common aspirations of L2 learners around the world. We refer to a *degree* of fluency: how fluent learners need to become will depend on their personal goals, achievement levels, and attitudes but may also be dictated by institutional demands.

PERSONAL REFLECTION

Think of an occasion when you had to speak in a foreign language, such as in your schooldays or as a tourist. What difficulties did you face in speaking that language? Grammar? Vocabulary? Translation? Pronunciation? Keeping up with the conversation?

Fluency in a foreign language involves huge cognitive processing demands. You have to put your meaning into words by retrieving the most appropriate words from those stored in your mind for that language and arrange them coherently, exploiting the language's phonology and lexicogrammar, all in a matter of milliseconds. It is the mirror image of listening. The moment you speak, you have to pronounce and stress the words so that they are intelligible and connected, and most challenging of all, you have to contribute to the content and the general flow of the conversation. To be perceived as fluent, language should *flow*, whether fast or more slowly. Being fluent does not always mean talking fast. What matters is contributing to the flow, alternating as speaker and listener with your interlocutor(s), creating what McCarthy (2010b) calls **confluence**, as when two rivers flow into one.

INFORMATION ADD-ON

Flow and *fluency* are related in meaning; the adjective *fluent* comes from the Latin verb *fluere*, meaning to flow.

It can be difficult to give everyone equal opportunities to speak extensively in large classes, where speaking time per student may be severely rationed. Few learners will spend much time producing long monologues, but we can approach speaking as an individual, personal skill while not forgetting that the task of sharing the conversational flow involves interaction. In Chapter 8, we will consider how technology can give individual learners opportunities to practise speaking.

A distinction is often made between **fluency** and **accuracy**. Fluency entails putting meanings into words coherently, automatically, not disjointedly or too hesitantly. Accuracy is concerned with adhering to linguistic conventions. It is good practice that classroom time should be devoted sometimes to accuracy, sometimes to fluency. A focus on fluency may mean temporarily ignoring lexicogrammatical and phonological problems and giving learners uninterrupted freedom to talk. When accuracy is the focus, there may be a need for corrective feedback, remedial work, repeating, revising, and recasting features of production.

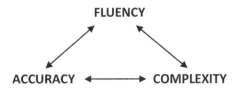

Figure 2.3 The fluency–accuracy–complexity triangle.

A third challenge is **complexity**. Complexity includes using grammatically sophisticated patterns, varying vocabulary, and expressing complex meanings. Complexity competes for attention with fluency and accuracy, and, as one scholar puts it, 'trade-off effects impact language performance' (Vercellotti 2017: 92). In other words, paying attention to accuracy while speaking may affect fluency, with unnatural pauses and hesitation. Equally, complexity and accuracy may be in competition with each other (Figure 2.3). Such pressures are also involved in the writing skill, but real-time speaking places greater processing demands on the learner, with little or no time to plan, revise, or reflect during production.

TELL ME

Reports and narratives are the most straightforward and familiar ways that learners can be given opportunities to speak for an extended time in class. The simplest reports are where learners talk about their lives outside of class, their spare-time interests, their families/friends, what they do/did at weekends, and so on, told in pairs, groups, or to the whole class. From pairs and groups, report-back sessions can be held. The teacher can take a back seat while learners perform (Figure 2.4) or can circulate and monitor what students are saying, though this can be off-putting or intimidating if too obvious and overbearing. Such reporting activities can be fluency focused and made more interactive by encouraging students to ask each other relevant questions.

Students can also record themselves on phones or other devices if available (see Chapter 8 on mobile learning), giving short personal reports. However, in large classes, this can place a considerable burden and time pressure on the teacher; in that situation, it may not be possible to give more than general, holistic feedback on a learner's performance.

Figure 2.4 Reporting in the classroom.
Source: Image © Áine Walsh 2023.

Reports of experiences, stories, and anecdotes are universal human activities. They are a familiar context for the development of speaking skills. Stories in the classroom can be anything from brief reports to longer, entertaining narratives if time allows.

Good stories have a structure; they are not just a random string of events. The sociolinguist William Labov devised a model for oral narratives based on how stories regularly follow a pattern (Labov 1972). Stories typically start with an *abstract*, which sums up the whole story: (*I had a scary experience last week*). Then comes the *orientation*, which sets the scene: (*I was driving home from work. It was very windy*). If the speaker stopped there, we would say, 'Yes, so, what happened?' A story must have at least one *complicating action*, an event which is unusual, scary, funny, unexpected: (*Suddenly a tree crashed down on the road in front of me*). Now we want to know how things turned out, hopefully positively: (*Luckily, I was able to brake in time, so I was okay*). This is the *resolution* of the story. Then the storyteller typically gives an *evaluation*: (*It was scary, but I was very lucky*). After that, the teller can bring us back to the present with a *coda*, a bridge that links the story time with the moment of telling:

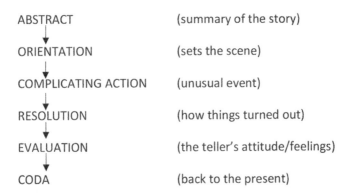

ABSTRACT	(summary of the story)
↓	
ORIENTATION	(sets the scene)
↓	
COMPLICATING ACTION	(unusual event)
↓	
RESOLUTION	(how things turned out)
↓	
EVALUATION	(the teller's attitude/feelings)
↓	
CODA	(back to the present)

Figure 2.5 Oral narrative structure (after Labov 1972).

(*I'll be more careful in future, especially if there's a high wind*). Figure 2.5 shows Labov's model diagrammatically.

Learners at lower proficiency levels can usually tell the bare bones of a story, providing some orientation, a complicating action, and a resolution. The abstract, evaluation, and coda tend to come later, when a greater command of the lexicogrammar is achieved. More advanced learners can be encouraged to fill out the story with these other elements where they are lacking. Telling the same story twice or three times, receiving feedback or evaluating their own performance after each telling, and adding more elements each time, for example, intensifying the evaluation (It was a *nightmare*, but I was *incredibly* lucky') builds story-telling skills.

Using Labov's model in language teaching is an illustration of why, in Chapter 1, we made a distinction between language at the level of lexicogrammar and phonology and language at the level of discourse. Exploring the narrative structure is an example of discourse-level teaching.

WHO'S LISTENING?

In this book, we stress the need to help learners develop *interactive* skills rather than just the skills of individual performance. In conversational storytelling, listeners do not usually take over and tell the main story, but they often ask for more orientation (*When was this?*) or share in the evaluation (*Wow! That sounds scary!*), and they may provide a coda (*Well, it's good you're okay*). At the very least, listeners provide feedback to show they are following the story, either by using vocalisations such as *mm* or *aha* or the responding items illustrated earlier in this chapter, such as *right* or *wow*.

CORPUS EVIDENCE

In this extract, <S1> tells a story of a trip to Japan and taking the Shinkasen (high-speed train). The listener <S2> constantly feeds back to the storyteller (items in bold).

<S1> I went we went to Tokyo with er the opera company <S2> **uhu** <S1> er but we had a bit of time off so I thought well I'm not hanging around in Tokyo, cos I'd been before and I'd seen quite a lot of it so <S2> **mm** <S1> I got on the Shinkansen and then <S2> **right** <S1> and went and I was, sort of, spoke to one of our interpreters and I said well where would you recommend? and he said well everyone goes to Mount Fuji er <S2> **yeah** <S1> I went I don't wanna go anywhere where <S2> **no** <S1> the tourists go <S2> **no no** <S1> I wanna go somewhere which is different so I went right the way across to the other side of Japan <S2> **yes** <S1> to <S2> **yeah** <S1> to erm Sado <S2> **yeah** <S1> the other end of Sado? <S2> **right yeah** . . .

(Spoken BNC2014 S263)

In the Corpus Evidence box, the listener is not heard as interrupting the story. Giving verbal feedback is normal, and transcripts of storytelling usually look as much like dialogue as monologue. When learners are in pairs or groups reporting or telling stories, whoever is in the listener role can be encouraged to show good listenership.

However, speakers also have to think constantly of the people they are addressing and adapt their talk appropriately. This two-way relationship leads to what sociolinguists call **audience design**, the style we adopt when addressing others. As the sociolinguist Allan Bell put it: 'speakers take most account of hearers in designing their talk' (1984: 159).

MIND THE GAP

A basic technique for encouraging interactive speaking is **information gap** activities. These work on the principle that a pair or group of learners share some, but not all, the information on a given topic, which often happens in the world outside of the classroom. An example is a role-play where students must organise travelling to a concert and have a meal together before going to the venue. One student has information about the time and place of the concert; another has train and bus timetables; a third has a map showing stations, bus stops, and restaurants. The group negotiates the best way to get to the venue, what time to meet up and travel, where to eat, and so on.

Information gap activities often rely on complex language exchanges and so may work best with higher-level students. Simpler versions of information gap can be devised, for example, two simple maps showing a small number of places (e.g., station, theatre, museum), some on one map, some on the other, and street names, where learners ask each other questions (Q: *Where is the museum?* A: *Park Street*). As with listening, there is a good case for a *before-during-and-after* approach to speaking tasks – activating schemata, feeding in useful vocabulary before the task, and evaluating the success (or failure) of the task afterwards.

THINGS TO CONSIDER

The fluency, accuracy, and complexity model, including features like good listenership, is suitable for adult learners in multilingual classrooms. But there are other factors which affect speaking skills, some of which Anne Lazaraton mentions in her survey of the teaching of L2 speaking. She recognises that multilingual classes may be better suited to fostering speaking skills, then goes on to say:

> However, homogenous EFL classes, where all students speak the same L1 and outside exposure to English is limited, present certain additional challenges for the teacher of L2 speaking including motivation, the use of the first language, and getting students to speak (especially in cultures where speaking in class is prohibited unless called on).

> (Lazaraton 2014: 116)

Another factor is proficiency level, especially the beginner level. Here Jonathan Newton and Paul Nation suggest working on very basic elements such as saying the alphabet, simple vocabulary and common phrases (2020: ch.2). Age is a factor, too. When we look at young learners in Chapter 3, we will see what some of the pros and cons are if you are just 8 or 12 years old. Also, learners who need English for academic or professional qualifications may require more specialised speaking activities to prepare them to give presentations, take part in meetings, seminars, and so on.

READING

WHY READ?

William Grabe and Junko Yamashita say:

> Students may learn to read an L2 as a school subject with little further use outside the classroom. However, many students use their L2 reading skills to engage in advanced studies, get a good job, travel, gain access to information, become more cross-culturally aware, communicate with others, or be entertained.

(2022: 7)

For learners living in an English-speaking environment, signs, adverts, product names, and other public texts will catch their eye. However, learners coming from first language backgrounds with writing systems different from English may struggle in the initial stages of reading English and need practice in letter and word recognition and training in sound–spelling associations.

Reading is usually a silent activity, but that does not mean it is passive. It demands active engagement with texts. The text mediates interaction between writer and reader. When we read, we usually have a purpose, whether entertainment or pleasure (a novel, a poem), enlightenment (knowledge, education), or retrieving information (instructions, travel details). Reading is often embedded in tasks involving other skills. Reading in educational settings often has the purpose of notetaking, and in daily life, we often speak about what we have read or read instructions to complete a task (Figure 2.6).

Figure 2.6 Reading with a purpose.
Source: Image © Áine Walsh 2022.

PERSONAL REFLECTION

Think of what you have read in the last seven days. Why did you read those things? For entertainment or for other purposes?

Neil Anderson talks about 'engaged' second language readers and lists five characteristics, summarised here. Engaged readers:

- read widely with varied purposes.
- read fluently and focus on meaning.
- develop comprehension.
- are aware of their use of reading strategies.
- are motivated.

(After Anderson 2014: 171)

The language class can offer different types of texts for different purposes and assist learners to achieve the characteristics listed by Anderson. Narrative texts (e.g., short stories) usually alternate with **expository** texts (texts that provide facts and information).

The second characteristic of a good reader listed previously is the ability to read fluently and to focus on meaning. Fluent reading means reading sequentially and smoothly. Words have to be processed quickly and automatically. However, meaning will rarely reside in each single word but will be a cumulative process of relating words to one another syntactically, decoding collocations, recognising chunks, and using punctuation, with the eye sometimes fixed on a word, sometimes hopping forward, sometimes looking back in the text. This bottom-up processing of the text is important, but there will inevitably be gaps where insufficient knowledge of vocabulary and grammar will impede the flow. That is where top-down processing comes into play, with guessing, prediction, and inference coming to the fore, as well as prior world knowledge and **textual schemata** such as the problem-solution template illustrated in Chapter 1 (Hudson 2007: ch.7). Flexible movement between bottom-up and top-down strategies underpins comprehension. When we read efficiently, we monitor our comprehension moment by moment and make mental adjustments as we move through the text (Grabe and Stoller 2018: 13). Sometimes we just need to find one piece of information buried in the text, and the best strategy may be to **scan** the text looking for key words or key headings. Equally, we may want to get a general idea of the gist of the text before deciding whether it is useful or whether to read it in greater depth, in which case we **skim** over the text to get the main points. **Scanning** and **skimming** are two key reading strategies. Jim Scrivener, in his comprehensive guide to ELT, offers classroom tasks to foster top-down reading skills (2011: 263–268).

Most beginner learners of English as an L2, including young learners, will have some experience of reading in their first language, and we can assume that whatever skills and strategies they have acquired in their L1 can be carried over into L2 reading (Nation and Macalister

2021: 4). However, a lower-level learner with a smaller vocabulary will have greater difficulty in reading a text and employing useful strategies. Some researchers have suggested that for academic reading, it may be necessary to understand between 95 and 98% of the words in a text to achieve full comprehension (Schmitt et al. 2011). Even with 95% comprehension, as many as 1 in 20 words may be new, and this can make top-down inferencing and other strategies difficult to implement. Nation and Macalister (2021: 12) say: 'Learners should read with 98 per cent coverage of the vocabulary in the text so that they can learn the remaining 2 per cent through guessing from context'. This is a high demand which requires starting with simplified texts, providing glosses of difficult words and phrases, strategic use of dictionaries, and support from the teacher or from peers in reading groups.

RESEARCH EVIDENCE

Vocabulary knowledge is a key to proficiency in L2 reading and is a reliable prediction of a reader's competence. Learners who scored higher on vocabulary tests achieved higher comprehension of selected reading passages. See the studies by Schmitt et al. (2011) and Qian (2002).

TEXTS: EASY OR HARD?

Grappling with an extended text in a second language is different from reading a sign or a short social media posting, but 'difficulty' depends on many factors, some linguistic and some related to the learners themselves. Texts which are dense in vocabulary will pose more challenges. 'Dense' vocabulary can be formally measured in terms of **lexical diversity**, which is a measure of the lexical (as opposed to grammatical) words in the text. If the text has many *repeated* lexical words, it will have lower lexical diversity, and vice versa; texts with a great number of *different* lexical words may be more difficult to process, because greater lexical diversity will also affect the complexity of meanings in the text. The level of complexity and difficulty will be further increased if the text is both long and lexically diverse.

Online tools for measuring lexical diversity and text difficulty are available. One tool is *Text Inspector* (https://textinspector.com), which enables you to upload a text and get a statistical measure of its difficulty based on features such as lexical diversity, word length, and sentence length.

TEXTS: KEEP IT SIMPLE?

If texts are too difficult, there are various options. One is to simplify them or to create texts with limited vocabulary, such as the graded readers that publishers put out for various levels of proficiency. Other options include providing vocabulary before reading, glosses of difficult words on the page during reading, or to encourage learners to use dictionaries. All of these have advantages and disadvantages. Simplified texts and graded readers may motivate learners not to give up but may not push them beyond their comfort zone towards new learning challenges. Vocabulary glosses may help to maintain motivation but may not lead to lasting acquisition of vocabulary, which is a major factor in achieving reading proficiency. Dictionaries, if over-used, may hinder the 'flow' of reading (Laufer 2013). As always, maintaining a balance is best practice.

Learners can be encouraged to re-read the same text as a way of consolidating comprehension, with considerable bottom-up work and relevant tasks along the way, that is to say **intensive reading**, but this may not be as effective as **extensive reading** on broad topics of interest done for enjoyment. The British Council's *Teaching English* website says of extensive reading:

> Learners can be encouraged to read extensively by setting up a class library, encouraging review writing, and incorporating reading of books into the syllabus, and dedicating some class time to quiet reading.
>
> (www.teachingenglish.org.uk/article/extensive-reading-0)

Jeremy Harmer lists many different reading sequences for the classroom (2007: 283–302).

WRITING

PENS AND KEYBOARDS

Learners' needs vary when it comes to writing. Young learners may be simultaneously grappling with learning to write in their L1 and

L2 English; young adults may need to develop academic and professional/vocational writing skills to support their education towards a career. Other adults may need to write English in the context of *lingua franca* business and professional situations or may practise writing as an element of general English courses focusing on leisure-motivated learning.

Where and when we write generate different types of texts: academically oriented students may have to write essays, lab reports, articles, literature reviews; school students may write essays on set topics for exams; young learners may write stories or dialogues (see Chapter 3); people may write social media posts in English, complete official forms, or make travel reservations. Writing can be done on a keyboard, in handwriting, or through voice-to-text software. As with the other skills, two features are paramount: purpose and interaction.

Much that can be said about speaking is true about writing. Both skills involve fluency, accuracy, and complexity. Speaking and writing share the process of putting meanings into words. Writers, like speakers, have to choose the most appropriate words for their intended meaning, make lexicogrammatical choices, and assemble coherent stretches of language that communicate the message effectively to the receiver. However, there are differences.

TIME DELAY

One difference between speaking and writing is that writing is seldom experienced by the reader at the same moment that it is written; typically, there is a time-gap. An essay may be read by an examiner days after its creation, a social media post can stay online for days, weeks, months, with readers coming to it at various times. We hope that this book attracts readers for several years. This time-lag has consequences for writing skills:

- The reader may be unknown to the writer; writers often have to 'imagine' the reader.
- The writer has time to compose, revise, and edit the text before completing it.

PERSONAL REFLECTION

Think of something you have written recently. Who was the intended reader? What was your purpose in writing it? Where did your text end up: Online? With a teacher/tutor? As personal notes for an essay? A shopping list?

AUDIENCE DESIGN

Good writers write with readers in mind. In the English language classroom, the reader is often the teacher, and learners design their texts with the teacher in mind. This is not a bad thing, because interacting with one's teacher is one of the mainstays of getting on in the target language. Feedback from the teacher is a natural and rewarding process. However, other possibilities exist: a learner's target reader can just as well be another learner, a group, or the whole class. Audience design can break out of the classroom, with learners practising writing posts for social media, blogs, personal statements, and CVs for applications to educational institutions. In each case, mentally picturing the reader, putting oneself in the reader's shoes, is essential. The text is a vehicle; its purpose is to mediate between writer and reader; the goal, as always, is successful interaction.

Audience design includes structuring the text coherently. In a narrative, the order of events must be clear, as well as who did what, how, and why. The narrative model put forward by William Labov discussed under the speaking skill is just as useful in writing. A good written narrative guides the reader through time and events and includes signals and signposts. **Signals** alert the reader to what is happening in the text (e.g., *There are two possible **solutions** to this problem*). **Signposts** help the reader navigate their way through the text (e.g., *first of all; the next thing that happened*), just as signposts guide people around the landscape. As with oral narratives, beginner and young learners may not be ready to exercise all the features of narrative design, but writing simple stories is possible from the early stages.

In expository texts, structures such as the problem–solution pattern discussed in Chapter 1 can be exploited. In problem–solution texts, typical vocabulary signals of the 'problem' element are *problem, issue, challenge*, while solutions can be signalled with words such as *result, outcome, solution, resolution*, with other vocabulary signalling evaluation (*successful, effective, ineffective*).

Adult learners will already have experience of narratives from their L1, but other rhetorical patterns may prove more challenging (e.g., argumentative essays comparing and contrasting standpoints). Awareness of more complex expository templates may have to be taught explicitly. Ken Hyland gives examples of different expository templates. He also points up different approaches to understanding and teaching the writing skill, none of which need be seen as exclusive (Hyland 2019: 3).

PRODUCT AND PROCESS

So far, we have looked at two types of texts and how they are designed for readers. We could also take a bottom-up approach and consider how learners deal with the lexicogrammar of sentence creation. This might include awareness of different degrees of formality (academic essay versus friendly email) or punctuation and conventions of formatting (see Hinkel 2006). Hyland describes the sequence of activities that might result from this approach, including pre-teaching of grammar and vocabulary, controlled writing (where learners manipulate structural patterns), through guided writing (where learners imitate model texts) to free writing (Hyland 2019: 4). In this way, creating a text is centred on building with language.

Another approach takes the emphasis off the text as a product and looks at the stages which writers can take their texts through before considering them finished, a **process writing** approach. A piece of writing is planned, beginning with brainstorming of ideas, followed by a rough draft, followed by review, revision, and editing until the final product emerges. Jeremy Harmer notes that this is how experienced writers write (2004: 4–6). The process is non-linear and can loop around in various ways, repeating some stages, reacting to feedback to rough drafts, refining accuracy and complexity. Figure 2.7 illustrates this.

Figure 2.7 shows how the familiar concepts of complexity, accuracy, and fluency play a role in the process: the finished text should flow, just like fluent speaking. One final parallel can be drawn

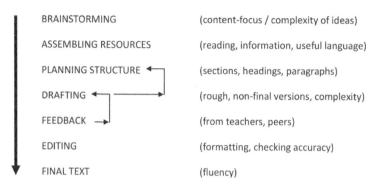

BRAINSTORMING	(content-focus / complexity of ideas)
ASSEMBLING RESOURCES	(reading, information, useful language)
PLANNING STRUCTURE	(sections, headings, paragraphs)
DRAFTING	(rough, non-final versions, complexity)
FEEDBACK	(from teachers, peers)
EDITING	(formatting, checking accuracy)
FINAL TEXT	(fluency)

Figure 2.7 Process writing.

between writing and the other skills. Extensive reading, done for pleasure, can be a powerful source of language development. Free, creative writing can serve a similar purpose, with learners putting their personal worlds and experiences into words, a process involving grappling with language, mental organisation, and audience design, but whose primary purpose is self-expression.

THE FIFTH SKILL

We conclude this chapter by reiterating our main theme, interaction with our fellow human beings. It is why we speak and listen; it is why we read and write. The conventional four skills are best considered as sub-skills of the main, most purposeful of skills: successful interaction. Let us call interaction **the fifth skill**. You will find other mentions of a 'fifth skill' in language learning if you search websites. Some see it as intercultural communication; others see translation as the fifth skill. As a teacher, you may find yourself teaching aspects of culture or working in contexts where translation is important. In this book, we reserve the term *fifth skill* to refer to the intertwining of the conventional four skills to develop **interactional competence** (Kramsch 1986). The classroom is the nerve-centre of this intermingling of skills and teachers help learners navigate the complexities of language learning (see Chapter 6). But first we take a closer look at learners themselves.

FURTHER READING

Harmer, J. 2004. *How to Teach Writing*. Harlow: Pearson Education Limited.
Jeremy Harmer's book covers the process of writing, from text types to the ways experienced writers compose their texts and practical matters of teaching handwriting, spelling, and punctuation to tasks for the classroom.

Jones, C., Byrne, S. and Halenko, N. 2018. *Successful Spoken English*. Abingdon, Oxon: Routledge.
Chris Jones and his co-authors use extensive learner corpus evidence to examine spoken competence. The book includes chapters on strategic competence, discourse competence, and pragmatic competence and covers themes from this chapter and others in our book.

Nation, I. S. P. and Macalister, J. 2021. *Teaching ESL/EFL Reading and Writing*. Second edition. New York: Routledge.
Paul Nation's book has a wealth of information, theoretical and practical, for teachers of reading and writing. It combines research evidence with teaching experience and covers areas touched on in this chapter such as fluency, intensive and extensive reading, and the writing process.

Newton, M. J. and Nation, I. S. P. 2020. *Teaching ESL/EFL Listening and Speaking*. Second Edition. New York: Routledge.
Jonathan Newton and Paul Nation's book is a guide to developing speaking and listening skills at all levels. It tackles issues explored in this chapter, including fluency, accuracy, and complexity, with different ways of focusing lessons, such as language focused or fluency focused.

3

THE MAIN ACTORS
LEARNERS AND LEARNING

WHO ARE OUR LEARNERS?

Learners are the main stakeholders, the reason we exist as teachers. No two learners are the same, but learners often share characteristics that influence learning, such as age, educational environment, needs, and goals. Here we explore some of those characteristics that enable us to group and distinguish types of learners.

AN EARLY START

Some educators regard **young learners** as anyone up to age 18, after which 18–25-year-olds are referred to as **young adults** Some measure the age-range of young learners from the earliest years to secondary school age, for example, 3–12 years old. **English for young learners (EYL)** in this age span requires a 'child-centred pedagogy rich in oral input and meaning-centred learning' (Bland 2015: 1). The chapters in Valente and Xerri (2022) cover a wide range of themes in EYL.

Children aged 3–12 have a natural curiosity towards the world around them; play, interaction with adults, and physical activity are key ingredients of the learning process. In those years children absorb their first language (or two languages in a bilingual environment).

INFORMATION ADD-ON

Little children can learn a first language at an impressive rate. McCarthy (2023: 106) notes:

DOI: 10.4324/9781003350316-3

At birth, a child knows no words. By age two, they are typically able to produce anything up to a thousand words (Nation and Coxhead 2021: 7). By age seven, the age when many children around the world start school proper, we can expect an English-native-speaking child to know about 5,000 word families.

At first glance, young children have an easy time of it, with play, physical activity, time, and adult support all providing a stress-free environment for language learning. However, L2 acquisition is complex. Adults may grasp the structural intricacies of a second language more quickly than children, while children usually acquire good L2 pronunciation more quickly than adults. The **critical period hypothesis** (**CPH**) claims there is an age span (debated, but perhaps up to 12 years old) during which the child's developing brain can acquire a second language with greater ease than after age 12, while pronunciation is facilitated by the greater adaptability of the child's vocal apparatus. Young children also rapidly acquire fluent L2 oral interactive skills (Cummins 1981). But children may struggle with the cognitive demands of learning to read and write. However, in the longer term, they can catch up regarding the more cognitively demanding aspects of L2 learning (see Collier 1987). We cannot generalise 100% about these differences. Some adults acquire near-native proficiency, and their motivation to learn may be stronger. The situation is complex, as David Singleton shows in his survey of age-related second language acquisition (Singleton 2001). The age at which English L2 education begins has become lower and lower; children starting English as young as three or four years old is not uncommon in some parts of the world.

NATALIA THE COMMUNICATOR

Natalia (not her real name), a refugee, arrived in the United Kingdom in 2022, aged eight, with her mother. She enrolled in an English primary school. She had received some elementary schooling in English in her native country and quickly acquired a basic level of spoken interaction in her new environment. Her mother had little or no background in English and began one-to-one

English lessons with a volunteer tutor. Natalia quickly acquired a more native-like accent than her mother and was uninhibited in speaking. She had acquired a basic English vocabulary and could unhesitatingly name different fruit, vegetables, and animals. She picked up a number of chunks such as *See you tomorrow, Where is x?, Can I have a/some x*. She developed simplified grammatical routines, for example, around learning the violin, such as *Which song I play now?*, and spoke without inhibition.

When asked to produce a piece of writing about her life in England, Natalia enthusiastically took pen to paper. Figure 3.1 shows what she wrote. She invented the fictional name for her village (*Horsea* – she likes horses).

Natalia has had to learn a new alphabet. She has some trouble with letter formation (*draunise* for *Brownies*, *camdrige* for *Cambridge*), punctuation, and spelling. Aspects of her spelling reflect the phonology of her first language, such as blending of /v/ and /w/ in *I liw* (*I live*). Disregarding those minor problems, we see that she effectively communicates things that are important to her: her new home, the garden, her violin, her school. Play and interaction with adults and her peer group are important factors in acquiring her new language.

Natalia gets extra English language provision at school but also learns *in the wild* (informally) in interactions outside of school. At the time of writing, she is making rapid progress in all the skills. She

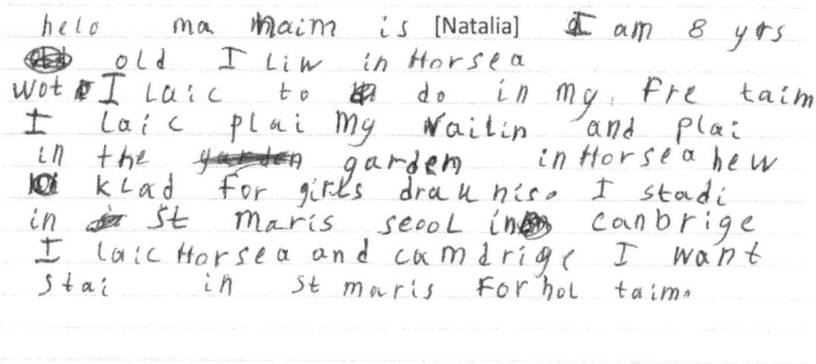

Figure 3.1 Natalia's composition.
Source: Image © Michael McCarthy 2023.

enjoys reading aloud and writing stories and dialogues. Here is one that she wrote (with her original spelling and punctuation on the left) and proudly read aloud, acting out different voices. She even wrote 'stage directions' (shown in brackets).

(qiuetley) Helo hello girls lets go to the thop	(quietly) Hello, hello girls, let's go to the shop. Yes. I'm really hungry.
Yes I rili hangre	(In the shop) Hello, hello, can I have a cake please?
(in te shop) Hello hello can I have a caic plis?	Yes! 25 pence please. Here we go.
Yes! 25 pands plis har we go	Thanks.
Sanks	Mm this cake is really nice.
mmm dis caca rili nais	I love cakes.
I love cacs	Me too.
mi too	Oh look, it's a big spider!
Ooo loke its a big spaider!	Oh no! A-A-A-A-A, I'm really scared of spiders.
O no! A A A A A I rili scerd of spaiders	Me too. Girls, look what I have.
Me two girls look wot I hawe	Yoho, it's a picnic, hooray!
Yoho its picnic huray!	
(reproduced by kind permission)	

Natalia's dialogue displays all the language-learning hurdles in her composition in Figure 3.1 (spelling, punctuation, simplified grammar), but she has the necessary vocabulary, and her composition reveals preoccupations of children her age: friends, shops, treats, encounters with scary creatures.

SCHOOL AND PEERS

Many young learners not living in English-speaking environments get their main exposure to English in school classrooms, where the number of contact hours may be limited. In monolingual environments, young learners can resort to their shared L1 when communicating in the classroom. This is evidenced in the spoken transcripts of the Barcelona English Language Corpus (BELC), an invaluable resource containing data from learners in the 10–18 age group performing written and spoken tasks (Muñoz 2006). The corpus includes short compositions where learners introduce themselves and give their name, age, and sometimes family details and/or describe things they like. The 10–11-year-olds produce fewer sentences than the 15–16-year-olds, but the same ingredients are there: personal details, home and family, things they like. The 17–18-year-olds engage in personal reflections about themselves, their education, and their aspirations.[1] A corpus of EYL data such as BELC offers insight not only into how learners expand their L2 knowledge but also how skilfully they communicate with limited language and how cognitive maturation is reflected in the increasing complexity of content during adolescence.

CORPUS EVIDENCE

This extract from the BELC shows two learners in the 10–11 age group performing a mini role play where one plays a mother and the other a youngster trying to arrange a party for their friends.

L20 and L60 are the learners. INV is the researcher. Codes show how the children speak; for example, the symbol '&' labels a hesitation (*uh*), [/] indicates repetition, and < > and [*] mark a language error. These codes enable scholars to search the corpus for useful information.

L20: &-uh hello mother.
L60: hello.
L20: &-uh <it's a party a house> [*].
L60: hm yes.
L20: (.) <it's> [/] <it's a (.) do a hundred invitation> [*].
L60: &-uh a hundred?
INV: friends.
L60: no.
L20: &-uh twenty <in> [*] friends.
L60: yes.
INV: good.
L20: &-uh (.) it's <a> [*] tuesday?
L60: yes.
L20: &-uh [/] &-uh three o'clock.
L60: yes.
L20: &-uh.

L60: no it's school.
L20: &-uh saturday it's <a> [*] four o'clock.

(BELC. Reproduced by kind permission)

Joan Kang Shin, in a survey of EYL, recommends that teachers take account of children's different learning styles, some being more visual and others learning more from auditory input (listening), while others benefit more from **kinaesthetic** learning, that is, moving around and touching objects (Shin 2014).

EYL involves games, role-plays, storytelling, drama, songs, physical activity, and so on, especially for the youngest learners. However, the transition from primary school to secondary school brings not only expanding horizons and the feeling of growing up but also anxieties and pressures. The language of the academic disciplines in secondary school poses challenges. For many youngsters around the world, this will include a more structured and cognitively demanding approach to learning English as a second language, The L2 English language materials secondary students work with are typically based on structured coursebooks, with longer texts and more new language on the page than simpler, heavily illustrated EYL materials.

IN AT THE DEEP END

Some children study everything through an L2. Early examples of this were Canadian **immersion programmes** in French from the 1970s onwards, reflecting the bilingual character of Canadian society. Some programmes begin as early as kindergarten, with 100% of learning happening through the L2. As the children move through the grades, a balance is struck between learning some subjects through French and some through English. Teachers deliver their lessons through each language as though their pupils were first-language speakers. One commentator says:

> Generally, immersion programs are designed to create the same kinds of conditions that occur during first-language learning; namely, there is an emphasis on creating a desire by the student to learn the language in order to engage in meaningful and interesting communication.

> (Genesee 1995: 124)

This is quite a different experience for young learners than typical second language lessons. The Canadian example has also been considered in a slightly different fashion in the United States (Lillie et al. 2012).

GROWING UP

CLIL

Many adolescent learners have the opportunity to learn some school subjects through English, a process called **content and language integrated learning** (CLIL). In this approach, school students in non-English-speaking countries may learn geography, history, or other subjects with English as the medium of instruction. As well as the twin goal of learning the school subject and learning English, CLIL aims to develop intercultural awareness. The authors of a book on CLIL say:

> CLIL is not a new form of language education. It is not a new form of subject education. It is an innovative fusion of both [and it provides] a more holistic educational experience for the learner.
>
> (Coyle et al. 2010: 1)

In CLIL, the fusion of content and language teaching gives greater exposure to the L2 than the traditional school timetable can offer; it supports cognitive development and interdisciplinarity. The difference between CLIL and immersion courses has been the subject of debate, and CLIL has been criticised for being poorly defined (e.g., Cenoz et al. 2014). There is a degree of overlap in contexts where school/academic content is accessed through English.

THE TEENS

Jim Scrivener, in his guide to ELT, lists the pros and cons of teaching teenagers. Pros include positive motivation, enthusiasm, a liking for organisation, and focus on things that are relevant for teenagers. Cons include emotional aspects of maturing, boredom, embarrassment, low motivation, and lack of discipline (Scrivener 2011: 328–329). Jeremy Harmer adds to these the need for peer approval and self-esteem (2007: 83). Both Scrivener and Harmer offer tips for teachers to get over problems. Scrivener suggests including project work, getting students to bring to class materials they want to work with, group work, and using up-to-date and relevant materials. Harmer also tackles problems of classroom discipline.

Late-secondary school students, usually around 16–18 years old, are about to enter the adult world. Many societies around the world see these years as a turning point in young people's lives.

PERSONAL REFLECTION

What dominated the later stages of your school education? Exams? Decisions for the future? Difficulties? Excitement? High motivation?

Although 16–18 is often set as the age when students make the transition to the world of work or to higher studies, language classes for young adults may be made up of individuals who differ greatly in their level of maturity. In 2022, the *New Scientist* magazine published an article analysing what it means to become an adult. Its author noted that the human brain is not one undifferentiated mass; different regions of the brain, controlling different aspects of life, develop at different rates. Some regions can go on developing well into our 20s (Sarner 2022). Learners are always individually different, though they may find themselves in the same classroom through having reached a certain legally defined age or with a particular proficiency level achieved through standardised tests or national/international examinations.

ADULT LEARNERS

PATHWAYS

As teenagers mature, decisions are made regarding their future. Education becomes channelled into different pathways – some choose **STEM** subjects (science, technology, engineering, and mathematics); some choose arts or humanities (e.g., literature, history). Others follow more vocational pathways (teaching, social work) or pursue professional studies (business, law). Others go straight into the world of work. Many school-leavers embark upon careers in which English plays a role. This can involve studying for a degree in an English-speaking country or study through English medium instruction (**EMI**) in a non-English-speaking country (see Taguchi 2014; Macaro 2018). Those pursuing vocational and professional careers may need to read material in English to keep up with global developments in their professions. Those entering the business world often need to use English as a lingua franca. At these different crossroads in people's lives, a general English course may not meet their needs.

A BUSY LIFE

Despite the academic and professional compartmentalisation of ELT, many adults continue to learn English as a leisure activity or, in the case of immigrants and refugees in English-speaking countries, as a language essential to daily existence and social integration. For leisure-oriented learners, travel and tourism, hobbies, and interests frequently act as motivation. Some may have family connections across countries and languages for which English is a valuable resource.

General English courses for adults abound. Publishers go to great lengths to provide material that reflects the interests of adults. At this level, too, learners often wish to provide their own material such as texts that have caught their eye and which may interest their classmates. Adults in daytime or evening classes are often busy people. Unlike school or university students, they have varied duties and responsibilities. They may come to class exhausted after a busy day, and tiredness can affect memory and make the cognitive burden of learning even greater. Having said that, and despite the claims of the critical period hypothesis, many adult general learners achieve a high level of competence in English.

INFORMATION ADD-ON

In 2013, the British Council published a survey of the global status of English. These quotes from the document underscore the wide range of learners and learning environments.

> 70 per cent of executives said their workforce will need to master English to realise corporate expansion plans, and a quarter said more than 50 per cent of their total workforce would need English ability.
>
> (p. 7)
>
> English has become the lingua franca of academia.
>
> (p. 7)

NATALIA'S MOTHER

Earlier, we looked at the English of eight-year-old Natalia, a refugee. She came to the United Kingdom with her mother, Elena (not her real name). Elena had hardly any knowledge of English on arrival, but she immediately began one-to-one lessons with a volunteer experienced English language teacher. They meet several times a week at the teacher's home (Figure 3.2), fitting Elena's lessons around her job and child-caring responsibilities. They use a commercially produced general English language course.

Elena takes copious notes at her lessons and communicates effectively using her limited English. The teacher uses a small portable whiteboard to simulate a classroom atmosphere. In Figure 3.2, we see the teacher's whiteboard notes on countable and uncountable nouns (*eggs* versus *rice*), along with statements people make about diet.

Elena was also keen to write. Like her daughter Natalia, she wrote a short composition on the village that is their new home (here anonymised to *Lofton*). Elena's composition (Figure 3.3), written eight months after her arrival in the United Kingdom, is impressive for someone so recently taking up English. There are several reasons for this: she is highly motivated, she is a learner who cares about accuracy, she is cognitively mature and highly intelligent. She is prepared to grapple with complexity. Above all, she is strategic. In more pressing oral situations, she uses simplified grammar. She relies on her phone as a dictionary and uses its translating function when necessary in both speech and writing. She uses technology to her advantage but also puts a lot of effort into her learning.

Figure 3.2 Elena's English lesson.
Source: Image © Michael McCarthy 2023.

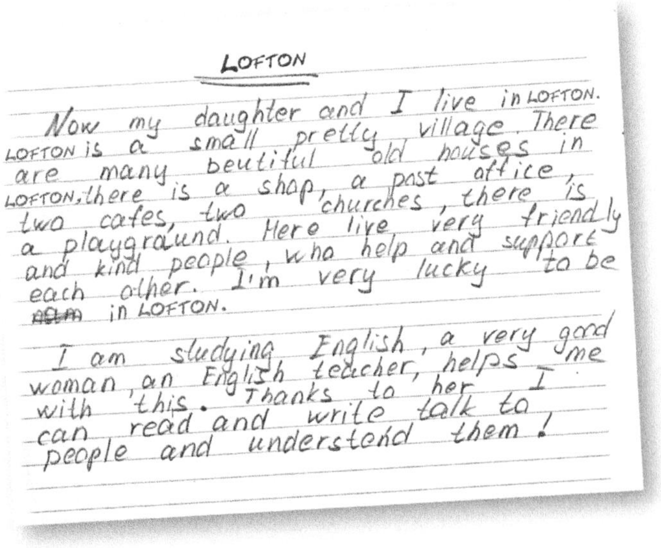

> LOFTON
>
> Now my daughter and I live in LOFTON. LOFTON is a small pretty village. There are many beutiful old houses in LOFTON, there is a shop, a post office, two cafes, two churches, there is a playground. Here live very friendly and kind people, who help and support each other. I'm very lucky to be in LOFTON.
>
> I am studying English, a very good woman, an English teacher, helps me with this. Thanks to her I can read and write talk to people and understend them!

Figure 3.3 Elena's composition.
Source: Image © Michael McCarthy 2023.

THE THIRD AGE

Upon retirement, people often take up activities which career-building or domestic responsibilities denied them in earlier years. Language learning is often taken up alongside greater freedom to travel.

One of the authors spent four years teaching groups of retired people, nowadays referred to as **third age learners**. The learners were motivated and curious to embrace the history and culture of English, not just the language. They attended class punctually and regularly and always did the homework. There were never any classroom discipline problems, group and teacher frequently met socially outside of class, and it was clear that the social element was important.

Third age learners often complain of how hard it is to remember things, blaming 'old age', yet all learners have problems remembering language which they have only encountered a handful of times. Older learners bring wisdom, world knowledge, and experience which can be positively exploited in the classroom. They may have already had experience of learning foreign languages and may also benefit greatly from sharing lessons with younger learners. The benefits can operate both ways.

RESEARCH EVIDENCE

Research suggests that learning a new language in the third age can boost cognitive abilities and contribute to general well-being (Pfenninger and Polz 2018). Some studies show that age is less important as a factor in successful third-age language learning than the learning strategies that older learners adopt (see the papers in Gabryś-Barker 2018).

LEVELS AND LABELS

EFL? ESL?

So far, we have used the term *English as a second language* for all contexts in which people learn English when it is not their first or native language. However, many in the ELT profession distinguish between learners for whom English is a 'foreign' language and learners whose needs are more immediate, for example, immigrants and refugees. Learners who see English as a foreign language are referred to as **EFL** learners. For these learners, English may be an obligatory school subject, it may include English literature and/or translation, and it may be on a par with other foreign languages being studied.

For learners such as immigrants and refugees, however, English is more than a 'foreign' language; it is the language of their new home. It is a matter of survival and building social capital to take their place in the world of work, education, and community. These learners are often referred to as **ESL** (English as a second language) learners. Janet Eyring points out that adult ESL learners come from complex and varied backgrounds:

> Adult ESL learners may vary by age, ethnicity, educational background, literacy skills, occupation and educational attainment. . . . They can be different races and religions and have very different educational backgrounds, from no formal education to advanced degrees.
>
> (2014: 569)

The heterogenous, multilingual character of the ESL context demands a different approach to the typically more homogenous, monolingual groups of learners in EFL school classes. ESL learners reflect shifting patterns of global mobility and multicultural societies (see Burns and Roberts 2010 for a discussion). They often have diverse experiences of language learning and previous education, and the length of residence in the new country also affects their learning. They may experience greater pressures outside of class while forging an identity in a new society; some may be traumatised by being uprooted and dropped into an alien environment. They may struggle to integrate conversationally and form social relationships (Taylor-Leech and Yates 2012). In the classroom the balance between fluency, accuracy, and complexity may need adjustment. For example, fluency in English in the workplace is crucial to success and economic advancement.

RESEARCH EVIDENCE

Two researchers, Barry Chiswick and Paul Miller, have shown in studies which include evidence from the United States, Canada, and Australia that there is a link between immigrants' achievement of proficiency and fluency in English and earnings in the workplace (2003, 2015).

In this book, we will continue to use the phrase *English as a second language* when referring to the general context of EFL/ESL, since in some respects the two share more than what divides them. The distinction is often blurred in the lives of individual learners: a businessperson who uses English as a lingua franca in an international corporation every day may hardly perceive English to be a 'foreign' language. Likewise, ESL students have to tackle the four skills and face similar lexicogrammatical and phonological challenges to those faced by their EFL counterparts.

INFORMATION ADD-ON

In addition to the sets of initials already discussed in this chapter, there is also **ESOL** (English for Speakers of Other Languages) and **TESOL** (Teaching English to Speakers of Other languages). In the United Kingdom, **TEFL** (Teaching English as a Foreign Language) is commonly heard; people often introduce themselves as a 'TEFL teacher' or say they are doing a 'TEFL course' to train as an English language teacher.

MORE PATHWAYS

School-leavers embark on different learning pathways if they need to use English in academic, vocational, and professional contexts. The needs of students at this stage become more clearly defined and specialised. Some take English courses to prepare for academic study under the heading of **EAP** (**English for academic purposes**).

EAP courses aim to give students the language and skills that underpin academic disciplines. As well as teaching the lexicogrammar shared across disciplines, EAP programmes usually cover essay- and report-writing, oral presentations, and interpersonal skills such as speaking in seminar groups. There may be a genre focus, for example, on the conventions of writing an abstract for an article or a literature review for a dissertation.

EAP courses place high cognitive demands on learners. Furthermore, they often bring together students from a range of different language backgrounds and academic disciplines. We authors have taught EAP to physicists, urban planners, engineers, historians, biologists, and business students, all in the same room at the same time. EAP materials writers therefore seek to find common elements across disciplines, ideally with the help of corpora (Viana and O'Boyle 2022). This sharing of the underpinning of academic discourse has a broader and longer-term benefit, too, since the current reality is that English is a lingua franca of global academic discourse (Mauranen et al. 2016), and cross-disciplinary scholarship has likewise grown in importance.

For specialised groups, **English for Specific Purposes (ESP)** may be more appropriate. An ESP class may consist entirely of urban planners, chemists, or marine biologists, for example. A **needs analysis** usually precedes the course (Flowerdew 2013). The analysis looks into what content the learners need to deal with through English, the discourse conventions of the specific discipline, and the learners' goals.

EAP and ESP overlap in many respects inasmuch as learners have specific needs, and there are common features of language and skills. One major handbook on ESP includes EAP as one of the 'SPs' and covers genre, dissertation writing, the use of corpora, and factors affecting a range of specialised English teaching (Paltridge and Starfield 2013).

Being an English language learner can mean many different things, some of which cross over the boundaries suggested by the various sets of initials and labels. Figure 3.4 attempts to capture such interrelations, but it is by no means the only way of conceptualising learners and pathways through English language learning. The diagram merely aims to sketch out the current complexity of ELT.

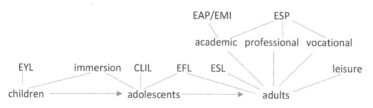

Figure 3.4 Learner domains and pathways.

MOVING THROUGH ABC

Teachers, caregivers, governments, educational institutions, and potential employers understandably want to know where language learners are on their learning journeys and so we also describe learners according to level of proficiency. To this end, the **Common European Framework of Reference (CEFR)** was developed under the aegis of the Council of Europe. The CEFR, when established in the early 2000s, consisted of three levels, A, B and C, each subdivided into two parts indicated by the numbers 1 or 2, thus A1, A2, B1, B2, C1, and C2. A1 is the lowest level of proficiency and C2 the highest. These very roughly correspond to the traditional levels of beginner/ elementary (A), intermediate (B), and advanced (C). Although 'European' in name, the system is used around the world.

The framework has undergone considerable revision, with online communication, young learners, and a pluralistic approach to culture and language now incorporated. However, the underlying principles remain the same: a set of **descriptors** or **can-do** statements of what learners are able to do with the L2 at various stages of their learning (Council of Europe 2020). The system *describes* typical learner profiles for each CEFR level. It was never intended to be prescriptive (stating what learners should or must learn), though the danger of prescription occasionally rears its head. The Council of Europe says of the framework:

> Its 'can do' definition of aspects of proficiency provides a clear, shared roadmap for learning, and a far more nuanced instrument to gauge progress than an exclusive focus on scores in tests and examinations.
>
> (2020: 27)

A simplified version of the CEFR levels for oral production is shown in Table 3.1, with quotations from the Council of Europe (2020: 62). This is one of many different sets of can-do statements; others cover different skills, and all can be found in the same publication.

CAN-DO AND CORPORA

Two resources freely available for consultation online, based on corpora of learner English production from around the world, describe what language is typically available to learners at each

Table 3.1 Simplified version of CEFR oral production skills.

Level	Learners . . .
A1	'Can produce simple, mainly isolated phrases about people and places'
A2	'Can give a simple description or presentation of people, living or working conditions, daily routines. likes/dislikes, etc.'
B1	'Can reasonably fluently sustain a straightforward description of one of a variety of subjects within their field of interest'
B2	'Can give clear, detailed descriptions and presentations on a wide range of subjects related to their field of interest'
C1	'Can give clear, detailed descriptions and presentations on complex subjects'
C2	'Can produce clear, smoothly flowing, well-structured discourse with an effective logical structure'

CEFR level. The **English Vocabulary Profile** (**EVP**) provides searchable lists of words and expressions learners can be expected to have a command of at each level (Capel 2015), while the **English Grammar Profile** (**EGP**) describes the grammar items and structures found at each level (O'Keeffe and Mark 2017).

RESEARCH EVIDENCE

The EGP distinguishes between *forms* and *use*. An example given by EGP researchers Anne O'Keeffe and Geraldine Mark shows what learners at B1 level can typically do with the English past perfect simple form. B1 learners can handle the affirmative form 'with a limited range of adverbs (including *never, ever, just, always, already*)' and can use the forms 'to talk about a time before another time in the past' (O'Keeffe and Mark 2017: 476).

The EGP also shows how learners develop pragmatic competence as they move through the CEFR levels, for example using the past simple form for making polite requests.

HOW DOES IT HAPPEN?

ACQUISITION

One ELT 'basic' we have not yet addressed is *how* learners learn: what the processes are whereby someone can acquire a vocabulary of several thousand words and a sophisticated command of grammar and pronunciation in an L2.

We know a lot about how little children acquire their L1. They spend a long time absorbing the language they hear in interactions with caregivers. Soon they start to produce sounds to express their needs and experiences (Halliday 1975). Next, they acquire chunks and words, followed by simple grammar, gradually acquiring a vocabulary of thousands of words and an effective command of grammar even before they start school.

However, L2 learners study English as a new language on top of the language or languages (if they are bilingual or multilingual) they already know. And they mostly do it through lessons with a teacher, in classrooms or online, using materials designed to provide short-cuts to acquiring the new language. Even if they are also learning in the wild (e.g., immigrants, refugees), the same questions apply: How does it happen? How do they learn? How does it stick?

PERSONAL REFLECTION

If you have learnt a second or foreign language, how much of it was conscious (e.g., learning lists of words and practising 'the rules') and how much could be attributed to unconscious processes while using the language?

ALL IN THE MIND?

Animals can be taught to do tricks. They perform for their keepers in return for rewards, usually food or a pat on the head. In human learning, we repeat something until we get it right and it becomes automatic. If you have done a language course where you repeat things many times and learn things by heart, you will know that, to an extent, the process works. You learn and remember grammar patterns and vocabulary and please the teacher/pass exams (the pat on the head). The right behaviour produces rewards; this is a **behaviourist** approach to learning.

Behaviour can be observed from the outside, but it tells us little about what goes on inside people's heads. A different way of explaining language learning is to think of humans as 'hard-wired' to acquire languages – a unique ability that separates us from other animals. This theory is associated with the linguist Noam Chomsky, who dismissed behaviourist explanations as being unable to account for language acquisition. Chomsky says:

> The fact that all normal children acquire essentially comparable grammars of great complexity with remarkable rapidity suggests that human beings are somehow specially designed to do this.
>
> (1959: 57)

This innate ability tells us that any language will have ways of describing actions, events, and states in the world, that grammatical relations such as subjects and objects of verbs will be in some way expressible in the L2. There are underlying principles that all languages share, a **universal grammar**. The adult learner tackling L2 will go through similar processes to the child learning L1. Children learning L1 and adults learning L2 take place in very different circumstances, but in both cases, the learner receives input and hypothesises on the basis of it within universal constraints.

An adult L2 learner may suppose that, since *I worked* is the past tense of *I work*, *I drinked* is the past of *I drink*. But instead of saying 'the learner got it wrong', it is more illuminating to talk about **interlanguage**, a notion developed by Larry Selinker in 1972. Interlanguage attempts to account for the nature of a learner's language at any given stage. The learner is neither using L1 nor L2 but is using a *system* that does not fall outside underlying universal principles. Interlanguage includes over-generalising and transferring features from L1 (Selinker 1972) and seems to follow predictable paths, regardless of the learner's L1. A beginner's simplified English negatives such as *no like* may be followed later by *I no like*, before settling on *I don't like* (VanPatten et al. 2020: 10–11). This led some scholars to talk about a **natural order** of acquisition, independent of the learner's L1 and regardless of how grammar is taught.

Further input changes the learner's interlanguage and moves it more towards L2 conventions, but usage can become **fossilised** or reach a **plateau** after which the learner makes no progress and will never reach native speaker competence. But the fact that learners generally will never reach native-user level may not matter.

Millions of learners achieve a level of competence in English which serves their needs, especially in lingua franca contexts. As Vivian Cook puts it: learners are not 'failed native speakers' (1999: 195). A positive view sees learners as multicompetent language *users*. In a later article, Cook addresses learners directly:

> Do not see yourselves as failures always trying to be like native speakers; see yourselves as successes, achieving things as L2 users that are out of the reach of monolinguals.
>
> (2016: 187–188)

However, as always, we respect individual learners' choices, and any learner who is unhappy with the feeling of being stuck on a plateau has the right to expect the teacher and materials to help them off it.

SLA: HAPPENING OR DOING?

One question often asked by those working in the field of **second language acquisition** (**SLA**) is whether learners should be given opportunities to acquire language indirectly, through **incidental** learning, or whether learning should be **intentional** (Hulstijn 2013). This question is linked to the contrast between **meaning-focused** activity and **form-focused** activity. Meaning-focused learning happens when the learner engages in meaningful communication, acquiring language in the process. A strong version of meaning focus believes that all that is needed is **comprehensible input**, language that learners can already understand most of but which includes some new input to push acquisition forward, a theory referred to as the **input hypothesis** (Krashen 1994). Form-focused activity, on the other hand, 'involves attempts to intervene directly in the process of interlanguage construction by drawing learners' attention to or providing opportunities for them to practice specific linguistic features' (Ellis et al. 2001: 407). It is generally felt nowadays that a balance between meaning- and form-focus is best practice.

Another way of looking at SLA is to consider the learner's *output* when they *use* language to interact. Merrill Swain refers to this as the **output hypothesis** and says:

In speaking or writing, learners can 'stretch' their interlanguage to meet communicative goals. To produce, learners need to do something. They need to create linguistic form and meaning, and in so doing, discover what they can and cannot do.

(2000: 99)

Producing meaningful language (especially engaging in collaborative dialogue) does more than regurgitate input; it also enhances acquisition. Looking at language in this way takes us out of the invisible 'black box' of the mind into the social environment in which learning takes place.

CORPUS EVIDENCE

Researchers have turned their attention to how corpora can increase our understanding of SLA. Florence Myles provides a survey of learner corpus research in relation to SLA (2015).

LANGUAGE OUT THERE

A recent development in SLA research is **usage-based** approaches. In this view, acquisition parallels the degree of exposure the learner has to language in use. With sufficient exposure, the learner acquires the patterns and conventions of the language by a process of **induction** – drawing conclusions about meaning and function from numerous individual examples of use – while applying learning mechanisms not necessarily exclusive to language learning. Induction need not be a conscious process. This approach removes the need to theorise a hard-wired universal grammar and supports an **emergent** view of interlanguage as a continuously evolving process.

Nick Ellis and Stefanie Wulff explain emergent acquisition in terms of how often and in what contexts the learner experiences a pairing of form and meaning (2014). Usage-based SLA unites the natural proclivities of the human mind with external experience; acquisition is 'out there' as well as 'in there'.

A SOCIO-CULTURAL ANGLE

Probably the most widely used theory of theory of learning today is **socio-cultural theory** (**SCT**), which emphasises its social nature; learning takes place as learners interact with the 'expert' teacher. Learners collectively and actively construct their own knowledge and understanding by interacting with others. This is not to say that learning is a wholly social phenomenon. It is a combination of cognitive and social processes; as we said earlier, acquisition 'in there' and 'out there'.

The father of SCT is the Russian philosopher Lev Vygotsky. His theory stressed the way the mind is mediated, or assisted, by symbolic tools such as language. **Mediation** allows us to interpret and regulate our world; language is a kind of tool which helps us understand, question, acquire knowledge, and develop skills. Although Vygotskyan theory was originally used in the study of child and language development, it has relevance to L2 acquisition in the classroom (see, for example, Lantolf 2000).

SCT emphasises the social, dynamic, and collaborative elements of learning. Learning occurs in the first instance through interaction with others who are often more experienced. During this process, language is used as a symbolic tool to clarify and make sense of new knowledge, with learners relying heavily on discussions with the 'expert knower'. As new ideas and knowledge are internalised, learners use language to comment on what they have learnt; oral communication is used to transmit and clarify new information and then to reflect on and rationalise what has been learnt.

PERSONAL REFLECTION

SCT highlights the importance of language in learning; pretty well anything we learn to do involves the use of language.

Think about three things you have learnt in your life. Think of practical things like learning to play a musical instrument, drive a car, and so on. Think about HOW you learned and with WHOM. What role did language play? How did another person help your learning?

SCT holds that learning takes place in the **Zone of Proximal Development (ZPD)**. According to James Lantolf, the ZPD is a space for 'the collaborative construction of opportunities . . . for individuals to develop their mental abilities' (2000: 17). Applying this to language classrooms, we see how teachers and learners co-construct meaning through the give and take of classroom interaction. Learning occurs *in* the interaction, making an understanding of interaction central to effective teaching. The ZPD rests on the idea that any learning process can be broken into a series of interrelated stages and that learners need to be helped to progress from one stage to the next. This process of helping is known as **scaffolding**, the linguistic support given to a learner (Bruner 1990). For example, a teacher might feed in a specific word to help learners with a task or revise a specific grammar point. Scaffolding involves both challenge and support: challenge is needed to maintain interest and involvement, while support is needed to ensure understanding.

The amount of scaffolded support will depend on the evaluation by the 'expert' of what is needed by the 'novice'. In a classroom context, where so much is happening at once, such fine judgments can be difficult to make. Deciding to intervene or hold back in the moment-by-moment unfolding of classroom interaction requires sensitivity and awareness on the part of the teacher. These themes will be taken up again in Chapter 6.

CONCLUSION

In this chapter we introduced two 'basics': different types of learners and different ways of explaining L2 acquisition. The learner population is not static: socio-economic and geopolitical change means English language learners, at the time of writing, are different from the days when English was seen as a foreign language studied at school, as an academic subject in universities, or as a leisure pursuit. Those contexts persist, but learners now start much younger, and their needs and motivations as they mature increasingly reflect academic, professional, and vocational goals. Meanwhile, conflict and economic disparities have created new populations of migrant learners with pressing needs to integrate in English-speaking environments. At the same time, stakeholders have sought new ways of classifying learner proficiency.

The second 'basic' was a brief introduction to SLA, a field far wider than this introductory book can embrace. In SLA theory, new explanations periodically replace old ones. Despite uncertain conclusions, SLA research illustrates the complexities of language learning. In the next chapter, we look at the organisation of learning in syllabuses, methods, and materials designed to support acquisition.

NOTE

1 The BELC is accessible at https://slabank.talkbank.org/access/English/BELC.html.

FURTHER READING

Garton, S. and Copland, F. (eds) 2019. *The Routledge Handbook of Teaching English to Young Learners*. Abingdon, Oxon: Routledge.
This book contains articles by leading scholars on everything related to EYL, including CLIL, the critical period hypothesis, motivation, teaching methods, and teaching language skills.

Taylor-Leech, K. and Yates, L. 2012. Strategies for building social connection through English: Challenges for immigrants and implications for teaching English as a second language. *Australian Review of Applied Linguistics* 35 (2): 138–155.
This is article looks at learning strategies and how they are used (or not) by immigrants to maximise social interaction. Although focused on Australia, the article has much to offer anyone teaching ESL to immigrants.

Richards, J. C. with Pun, J. 2022. *Teaching and Learning in English Medium Instruction*. Abingdon: Oxon, Routledge.
Jack Richards is a teacher educator of vast experience, and all his books are worth following up. This book goes further into the domain of EMI in different contexts around the world than the present chapter has been able to.

North, B. 2014. *The CEFR in Practice*. Cambridge: Cambridge University Press.
Brian North has been involved in the development of the CEFR. He takes the reader through the framework in detail, how it was devised, the contexts in which it evolved, and its relevance to testing and assessment.

Gass, S. M., Behney, J. and Plonsky, L. 2020. *Second Language Acquisition: An Introductory Course.* **Fifth Edition. New York: Routledge.**
This book gives a comprehensive account of SLA approaches, theories, and methods, exploring the developments and trends we have briefly covered in this chapter, including learner corpora and other kinds of SLA data collection.

Lantolf, J. P. 2000. *Sociocultural Theory and Second Language Learning.* **Oxford: Oxford University Press.**
James Lantolf's book offers an analysis of every aspect of SCT. His position chimes with our attachment throughout this book to the idea that interaction is at the heart of language, communication, and language acquisition.

4

SYLLABUSES, MATERIALS, METHODS

ORGANISING LEARNING

When we learn something, we usually introduce a degree of organisation. If you pick up a guitar and learn to play without lessons or an instruction manual, you will probably tackle some of the basics – what note each string plays and how to shape chords; you probably won't offer your friends a concert on day one! As you practise more, you introduce further organisation, perhaps learning complex melodies and playing with others. Organisation serves two purposes: it enables us to learn more efficiently and to measure progress.

> **PERSONAL REFLECTION**
>
> Think of something you learnt successfully (e.g., sport, music, technology, art, or craft). How was your learning organised? What stages did it go through? What resources did you need?

CURRICULUM AND SYLLABUS

Many educational programmes and national education systems are based on a curriculum. A **curriculum** is a statement of the aims and scope of the teaching that is on offer. It is a high-level way of organising learning, often the key document in national education systems, and usually reflects an educational ethos. Such an ethos is reflected in the New Zealand school curriculum for English:

DOI: 10.4324/9781003350316-4

Students need to practise making meaning and creating meaning at each level of the curriculum. . . . As they progress, students use their skills to engage with tasks and texts that are increasingly sophisticated and challenging, and they do this in increasing depth.

(*The New Zealand Curriculum Online*: Learning Area Structure[1])

A curriculum does not tell teachers what they should do in class. In most institutions, learning is also organised around a **syllabus**. The British Council *Teaching English* website defines a syllabus in the following way:

A syllabus is a document that describes what the contents of a language course will be <u>and the order in which they will be taught</u>. The content of a syllabus <u>normally reflects certain beliefs about language and language learning</u>.[2] [our underlining]

The points we have underlined stress order and underlying beliefs. The syllabus derives its content and sequence from the aims of the curriculum and from theories and beliefs about language acquisition, all against the background of broader political, social, and institutional criteria (Figure 4.1).

ORGANISING A SYLLABUS

Teachers rarely get the chance to organise a whole syllabus; more often than not, this is dictated by governments, institutions, or teaching materials. However, understanding what goes into different kinds of syllabuses and the theories and beliefs that lie behind them is an ELT 'basic'.

GRAMMAR AT THE CENTRE

Some syllabuses are dominated in content and sequence by grammar and are termed **grammatical syllabuses**. The syllabus presents grammatical items and structures and includes headings such as verb tenses, articles, prepositions, modal verbs, and so on.

Grammatical syllabuses focus on forms and functions of the grammar, and, in strong versions, other areas, such as vocabulary and pronunciation, take second place. The order in which grammar

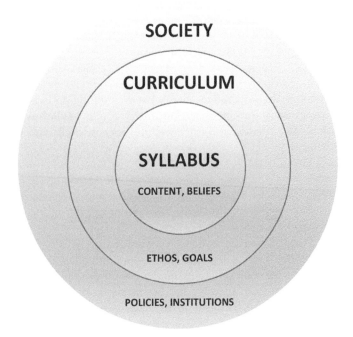

Figure 4.1 Society, curriculum, and syllabus.

features are presented may be based on intuition as to which forms are simpler and which more complex, so EFL/ESL syllabuses usually present the simple form of the present tense before the continuous and before past forms. If the syllabus writer subscribes to the 'natural order' of acquisition (see page 69), that may also affect the teaching sequence. Syllabus writers who believe that corpora give a more objective picture of the grammar people use may present features based on frequency, like the frequencies of the prepositions shown in Figure 4.2, which suggest prioritising *in*, *on*, and *at* before *through* and *between*. Within the top 30 prepositions in the spoken BNC1994, there is a great difference in frequency between *in*, *on*, and *at* and *through* and *between*.

Millions of learners have learnt, and continue to learn, second and foreign languages based on grammatical syllabuses. The upside is an orientation towards accuracy and engagement with increasing

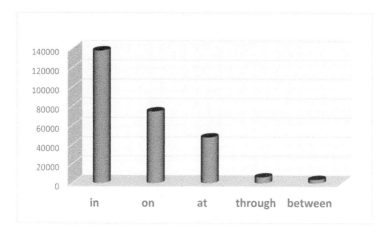

Figure 4.2 Frequency of prepositions.

complexity; the downside is that interaction, fluency, and creativity often take second place to the learning of 'rules'.

Traditional grammatical syllabuses see language as a set of structures; the learner's job is to practise and repeat those structures until they are internalised. For many decades, grammatical-structural syllabuses were the norm. Extract 4.1 is taken from a book for EFL beginner learners published in 1937; it looks old-fashioned now, but this type of syllabus lasted throughout the twentieth century in many parts of the world. The exercise requires a mechanical, form-focused processing of the reading passage. The philosophy behind the syllabus is that drilling structures and reading passages containing the structures are the way to learn grammar. The learners first read the passage; then they see the past ('imperfect') tense of the verbs *be* and *have* and finally must turn the reading passage into past tense.

EXTRACT 4.1

READING

This is my pencil. This pencil is mine. That is his book. That book is his. These are her pens. These pens are hers. Those are our copy-books. Those copy-books are ours. These are their grammars. These grammars are theirs. This one is mine. That one is yours. These (ones) are ours. Where are my books? Your books are here. Is this my pencil? Is that his copy-book? Are those our pens? No, they are not yours. They are hers.

Imperfect tense

To BE   To HAVE

Singular	*Plural*	*Singular*	*Plural*
I was	We are	I had	We had
You were	You were	You had	You had
He (she, it) was	They were	He (she, it) had	They had

Negative: I was not, etc. I had not, etc.
Negative-interrogative: Was I not? etc. Had I not?
Contractions: Hadn't I, wasn't I, weren't you? etc.

(Wenlock 1937: 6–7)

Modern grammatical syllabuses usually place more stress on grammatical features in interaction. For example, the first presentation of the simple past tense in a course co-authored by Michael McCarthy is embedded in reporting functions, including talking about your past week and remembering your first teacher/job (McCarthy et al. 2014a: vi).

EFL grammatical syllabuses led, over many decades in the pre-corpus era, to an unwritten consensus as to what they should contain, with, as Graham Burton puts it, 'not only strong agreement within the profession on overall grammatical content, but also on how this content should be split across levels' (2022a: 365). Burton suggests that the consensus was derived from common sense and experience-based notions of usefulness, learnability, simplicity, complexity, and so on but that such criteria are difficult to define objectively (2022b). The consensus has become a **canon**, an unwritten agreement on the set of items that ought to be in the syllabus. Anne O'Keeffe and Geraldine Mark refer to 'the ELT canon of grammatical structures. This is perceived as a "must-teach" list of items in an English grammar syllabus which has evolved over many years'

(2017: 466). O'Keeffe and Mark's and Burton's corpus-led critiques of the ELT canon have raised doubts as to its reliability.

CORPUS EVIDENCE

Corpus findings often challenge the canon and fixed ideas of grammatical features. McCarthy (1998: ch.8) gives the example of speech reporting using the past continuous form, for example, 'Mary *was telling me/ was saying* she's got a new job'. Corpora show that speakers often use these continuous forms to launch a new or interesting topic. Traditional grammar syllabuses typically focus on speech reporting with the simple form of the past ('Mary *told* me'/'Mary *said*') and omit the reporting function of the continuous form.

VOCABULARY

Syllabuses usually grade and sequence vocabulary in some way, and grammatical syllabuses often have parallel vocabulary syllabuses. Again, these may be created from intuition or experience, or what the syllabus-writer considers most useful for learners; they may be based on corpus evidence or a mix of input. For example, in one multi-level EFL course in circulation at the time of writing, the grammar of comparative and superlative adjectives is accompanied by a set of vocabulary which includes adjectives (*exciting, successful, sad*, etc.) and nouns (*comedy, thriller, documentary*, etc.) to support the grammar in enabling learners to talk about the comparative merits of different films (Puchta et al. 2022: 30–32). The grammar syllabus and the vocabulary syllabus are designed to work in harmony.

Corpora have played a role in the selection and ordering of vocabulary in syllabuses (e.g., McCarten 2007). It would seem sensible to include the most frequent vocabulary items first before moving on to less frequent ones. However, frequency is not like a gentle, downhill slope from the most to least frequent words: it is more like a steep mountainside, where, after the first 1,000 or so most common words, frequency falls off sharply and then flattens out; the rest of the vocabulary, amounting to tens of thousands of words, is relatively infrequent.

RESEARCH EVIDENCE

In another book in this *Basics* series, McCarthy shows how word frequency drops off sharply after the first 1,000 most frequent words in the Spoken BNC2014. The first 1,000 words account for 84% of the entire corpus, while the next 1,000 account for just under 4%, the third for less than 2%, and the fourth just 1% (McCarthy 2023: 25). A discussion on this phenomenon and implications for ELT can be seen in Paweł Szudarski's research (2018: ch.4).

Jeanne McCarten suggests that a vocabulary syllabus targeting the most frequent conversational items serves learners best, and a long-term goal of acquiring between 2,000 and 5,000 words is achievable (2007: 2). A central theme in this book is that learning English as a second language means acquiring interactional competence. The core vocabulary syllabus that grows from spoken data scaffolds acquisition and enables learners to learn through verbal interaction, as we mentioned in relation to SCT in Chapter 3.

THE LEXICAL SYLLABUS

Chunks are at the heart of the lexicogrammar of English (see Chapter 1). Corpus evidence reveals that everyday chunks are often as frequent as, or more frequent than, common single words. A vocabulary syllabus that reflects frequency of use ideally balances its content between single words and chunks. This relates to the need for exposure to examples of use considered essential in usage-based theories of acquisition (see Chapter 3); the most frequent chunks deserve a place in the language learners are exposed to. A syllabus that gives equal priority to words, word combinations, and lexical chunks is a **lexical syllabus**, distinguishing it from conventional, word-list based syllabuses (Willis 1990). For example, one current general English course highlights and gives practice for intermediate-level students in everyday vague language chunks such as *I think, kind of, sort of, stuff like that, things like that* (Latham-Koenig et al. 2020: 35).

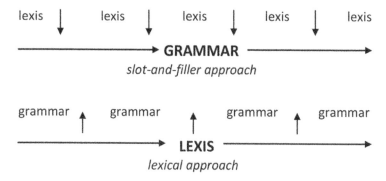

Figure 4.3 Slot-and-filler versus the lexical approach.

There is a fundamental difference between a lexical syllabus and a grammatical-structural syllabus. The grammatical-structural syllabus sees grammar as the foundation layer of language, offering 'slots' into which vocabulary is dropped – a **slot-and-filler** view of language. The lexical syllabus turns this on its head and sees lexical items and lexical chunks as the driving force in communication, with grammar seen as the after-trace of interaction (Figure 4.3).

Further underlining this contrast, John Racine says:

> While traditional approaches tended to present grammar constructions in order of ease of acquisition, lexis tended to be included based strictly on its relevance to the structures into which it was to be slotted. A lexical approach, informed by corpus data, provides language instructors with a principled means of introducing lexis into the syllabus.
>
> (2018: 1)

The lexical syllabus also deals with collocations (pairs of words with a high probability of occurring together) such as *strictly forbidden, steadily increasing,* as well as other word combinations such as compounds, phrasal verbs, and idioms. Corpus statistics are invaluable in assessing the frequency and usefulness of combined forms when building lexical syllabuses (for example, the syllabuses in McCarthy and O'Dell 2017a, 2017b, 2017c).

Strong versions of the lexical syllabus relegate grammar to the margins. Striking a common-sense balance between the memory-limited task of learning thousands of words and chunks and the cognitively demanding task of working out and applying the grammatical conventions is recommended practice. It is also possible that the acquisition of large numbers of chunks will have a side effect of fostering learners' grammatical awareness (see the discussion in Skehan 1998). For example, prepositional chunks reveal the regularity and productivity of the pattern preposition + noun-phrase (*at the moment, over the weekend, in a way*).

TAKEN TO TASK

The lexical syllabus was a reaction to the dominance of traditional grammatical syllabuses, but in the 1970s there was another kind of reaction which fundamentally upset the applecart. Applied linguists began to question whether a grammatical syllabus could serve the communication needs of learners, and **communicative language teaching** (**CLT**) was born. CLT took as its philosophy that language existed for *doing* things, for expressing **notions** (such as space, time, movement, etc.) and for performing **communicative functions**, giving rise to **notional-functional** syllabuses.

CLT grew partly out of the notion of communicative competence put forward by Dell Hymes, who believed that linguistic competence was more than a cognitive achievement and involved using language effectively in situations (1972). CLT was also based on **speech act theory**, the theory that all our utterances perform acts such as requesting, explaining, complimenting, apologising, giving permission, and so on (see the introduction to the theory in Cutting and Fordyce 2021: 14–24). It became clear that there was a mismatch between traditional grammatical explanations and communicative functions. The speaker who says *I'll carry that bag* may be offering to carry it or forbidding someone else from doing so. The offer or prohibition, depending on the context, is the **illocutionary force** of the statement.

Notions and functions cut across traditional explanations of grammatical features, and in the strongest version of notional-functional syllabuses, grammar was pushed down the list of priorities, even to the point of invisibility. A key figure in the communicative movement, David Wilkins, never dismissed formal features of the language but saw them growing out of the need to express notions and functions (Figure 4.4). Instead of going from form to meaning,

Figure 4.4 The notional-functional syllabus.

the starting point is meaning. Notions and communicative functions are mediated through situations to arrive at the appropriate forms of grammar and lexis (Wilkins 1976a).

The *situations/contexts* box in Figure 4.4 is concerned with:

> the language activities involved (i.e. reading, writing, speaking, listening), the likely situations of use, the domains in which the communication will take place, broadly the purposes to which the learners might be expected to put the language.
>
> (Wilkins 1976b: 7)

General English coursebook series soon adopted the idea of notions and functions and, from the 1980s onwards, they have formed a leading strand in syllabuses. The high-level *Viewpoint* series, for example, has *Functions/Topics* as a primary thread throughout the syllabus, framing the grammar and vocabulary threads and the threads for the four skills and conversation strategies (McCarthy et al. 2012: 4–9).

TASKS TO THE FORE

If language is all about *doing* rather than just 'saying', then it may also make sense to build a syllabus around the tasks people perform in which language is involved – a good part of anyone's daily existence. If we want the latest travel information, we visit a website or make a phone call; the goal is the travel information, and we achieve it through language. This principle led some applied linguists to argue for **task-based syllabuses** and **task-based learning** (**TBL**) (Candlin 1987). As David and Jane Willis put it, TBL 'involves the specification not of a sequence of language forms, but a sequence of communicative tasks to be carried out in the target language' (2001: 173).

In TBL, the stress is on achieving outcomes. In the task process, participants gather necessary resources, negotiate roles, carry out the task, and evaluate its success. All this happens collaboratively, involving teachers and learners. Tasks are seen as a series of procedures; some types of TBL syllabuses are referred to as **procedural syllabuses**, where the procedures, under teacher guidance, take precedence over language concerns but during which, it is asserted, language acquisition takes place. An alternative term is **process syllabuses**, where the learner's sense of needs has more say, where language focus is an option, and where the classroom and its activities are seen as the social setting in which the processes occur (Breen 1987: 166).

Task-based syllabuses are attractive in principle, but it is hard to see how the implementation of traditional syllabus-building principles such as itemising, grading, and sequencing of content can be consistently applied. On the plus side, TBL syllabuses offer flexibility and negotiability and allow for constant revision and adaptation.

A MIXED GRILL

Innovations in syllabus design have happened over the last half-century as views on the nature of language have evolved. Yet it would be a mistake to think that new waves successively wash away the old foundations. What mostly happens is that new types of syllabuses are bolted on to existing ones. At the time of writing, the **multi-strand syllabus** dominates in coursebooks and school curriculums. The typical multi-strand syllabus resembles Figure 4.5. Each strand is sequenced and makes a separate contribution to the learning process, but each strand is complementary to its neighbours.

Communication	Grammar	Vocabulary	Listening	Speaking	Reading	Writing
graded notions, topics and speech acts	graded items and forms	graded words, chunks and meanings	contexts, purposes, world varieties	genres: chatting, storytelling, dialogues	text types, reading skills, e.g. inference	text types, genres, skills
↓	↓	↓	↓	↓	↓	↓

Figure 4.5 A multi-strand syllabus.

The term **scope and sequence** is often used to refer to the structuring of the syllabus; we see the totality of what it covers (its scope) and in what order (sequence).

MATERIALS

MATERIAL ISSUES

ELT materials come in many forms. Generally, distinctions are made between **course materials** for use on programmes of study; **self-study materials**, which the user can work through out of class without a teacher; and **supplementary materials**, which can be used both in and out of class and which provide extra material to back up the main course materials.

The purpose of materials is to intervene in the acquisition process – to provide shortcuts in the otherwise lengthy process of learning a new language. The child learning their first language is immersed in the process and has the first years of life to absorb language during every waking hour. Most learners of second languages do not have that luxury and depend on courses and teaching materials.

Ivor Timmis sees materials as 'the instantiation of principles drawn from the broad fields of second language acquisition theory and language teaching theory' (2022: 30). In other words, materials and syllabuses go hand in hand in terms of shared principles and goals. Good materials are designed to achieve the goals of the syllabus. Multi-strand syllabuses are realised in multi-strand materials which generate activities and exercises designed and sequenced in line with the syllabus and its learning targets. TBL syllabuses may have a looser relationship to materials, with materials generated by the tasks on a more ad hoc basis, often sourced by the learners themselves in the service of the task.

Whether traditional grammatical, lexical, or TBL, the syllabus co-exists in an organic relationship with the materials. For example, in a TBL syllabus, unplanned materials may well be commandeered in the service of the task, but if they are disjointed from the overall syllabus goals of acquisition of language and/or skills, then the path to those goals may become more of a winding road than a shortcut. Figure 4.6 shows some aspects of the complex relationships between the syllabus and materials.

Figure 4.6 Syllabuses and materials.

Timmis proposes a set of principles for generating materials around the main language features and the four skills. For example, because fluent speaking is such a complex cognitive and social challenge, materials for teaching speaking should include scaffolding (see Chapter 3), such as controlled practice in vocabulary, before a speaking task is carried out. Another principle is that 'materials for speaking should raise awareness of features of spoken discourse' (Timmis 2022: 32–33).

CORPUS EVIDENCE

McCarthy, McCarten, and Sandiford include corpus statistics for raising awareness of spoken discourse in their coursebooks. In the advanced-level course *Viewpoint 2*, aimed at academically, vocationally, and professionally oriented learners, they give corpus statistics in a lesson on relative clauses, saying, 'Relative clauses with pronoun + *of whom/of which* are approximately 10 times more common in academic writing than in conversation' (McCarthy et al. 2014b: 63).

ARE THEY REAL?

One question that is regularly asked of ELT materials is: how far do they reflect the real world and the world of the end users?

Materials arise out of cultures and beliefs via the route we have described in this chapter – from society to curriculum to syllabus. One of the authors began teaching EFL over half a century ago using the Berlitz method. The method and textbooks were based on the ideas of its founder, Maximilian Berlitz (1852–1921). They were used across the world in language schools and continue to be used

(Thornbury 2011: 190). In the 1960s, the English coursebooks in use in Europe were rooted in British English and reflected the culture and values of a middle-class, well-to-do population and their language learning aims (travel, education, leisure), along with a form-focused structural, slot-and-filler approach. Extract 4.2 is an example of a reading passage aimed at illustrating the present perfect and past tense. It reflects a world where people have housemaids, where adult males are referred to as *Mister*, and where people send letters to one another:

EXTRACT 4.2

READING AND CONVERSATION

(A dialogue)

Mr. Miller: Mary, I hear the door bell ringing – Go and see who it is, please.

The maid: It is Mr. Jones to see you, sir.

Mr. M.: Please ask him to come in. Ah! good morning, Mr. Jones, how are you? Please sit down.

Mr. Jones: Good morning. I am very well, thank you.

Mr. M.: How long have you been back?

Mr. J.: I arrived yesterday.

Mr. M.: Did you get the letter I wrote you last Sunday?

Mr. J.: Yes, thanks, but I only got it on my return late last night.

(Berlitz 1966: 92)

The world has changed since 1966; the extract strikes us as quaint and amusing, and we would be very surprised to see modern materials portraying this social environment. The world of 1966 is an alien one for the vast majority of those learning English in the present day.

Materials writers nowadays usually work within norms set by publishers or institutions, and ELT materials are expected to conform to criteria which often include:

- Awareness of the learner population: is the target EFL, ESL, EAP, ESP, EYL, CLIL, third-age learning?
- Awareness of varieties of English, including national varieties and World Englishes.

- Multi-strand syllabuses based on communicative principles.
- Attention to learning styles.
- Illustrations that reflect geographical, cultural, and ethnic diversity.
- Avoidance of topics which might cause controversy, including religious and political issues.
- Sensitivity to users with disabilities (e.g., visual, aural).
- Gender balance and avoidance of stereotyping in texts and illustrations.
- Relevance: content and topics reflecting what people do and talk about.
- Corpus evidence to support language features, discourse types, and so on.
- Technological awareness: Will the materials be used online?

These norms reveal a broad awareness of present-day social and educational values in many parts of the world, but certainly not all, and many coursebooks overwhelmingly represent middle-class culture and values. What we can say with confidence is that our present-day ELT materials will be replaced by new ones which reflect the values of their time, and dialogues in current coursebooks will one day sound as quaint and outdated as Extract 4.2.

PERSONAL REFLECTION

If you have learnt a language using coursebooks and other material containing reading texts or dialogues, were you conscious as to whether the texts/dialogues felt natural or artificial and contrived? Did it matter to you?

Attempts at realism and present-day relevance are not the only criteria by which materials are judged. Much debate has also centred around **authenticity**. The common understanding of the term *authentic* is that it means real, genuine, not fake. Applying this to texts and dialogues in language coursebooks immediately raises questions. *Genuine*, in its strongest sense, would mean a text or dialogue written/spoken by someone with a real communicative purpose, to be read/heard by the audience it was designed for. This could, therefore, apply to the reading text and dialogue in Extracts 1 and 2 in this chapter. Both were written by professional material writers, addressed to real learners, with the purpose of offering them comprehensible input in the form of reading practice in English, an example of audience design. An exploration of this question is provided by Christian Jones in his article on authenticity in materials (2022).

This dilemma has led some scholars to exclude from the definition of *authentic* any text written for the purpose of language teaching. Yet problems remain. In presenting examples of genuine conversations, for example, the material writer might be faced with something like Extract 4.3, a not untypical transcript from the Spoken BNC2014:

EXTRACT 4.3

\<S1\> I enjoyed the day out
\<S2\> I I enjoyed you know
\<S1\> \<trans=overlap\>just being there and
\<S2\> the the trip
\<S?\> \<vocal desc=laugh/\>
\<S1\> the the kids at the front
\<S3\> \<trans=overlap\>it was alright it was an alright day out though wasn't it?
\<S2\> it was nice
\<S3\> \<trans=overlap\>it was a good day out and
\<S4\> \<trans=overlap\>yeah
\<S3\> a good little journey there

(Spoken BNC2014 S2K7)

This conversation meets one criterion for *authentic* in that it is a transcript of a naturally occurring conversation not designed for language learners. But plucking a spoken or written text out of its context leaves it hanging in space. In this case we wonder who these people are, what they are talking about, where they went on their day out. Without context, the conversation may come over as equally remote from the learner's reality as Mr Miller's conversation in Extract 4.2. We have to delve into the corpus, find out what we can about the people and what they were doing, then add contextual information before presenting it to learners. The speakers are in fact talking about a trip to see a football match. Not everyone cares about football. Perhaps that doesn't matter. What matters is the language – not too difficult, and just the sort of thing many people talk about. But can learners relate to this conversation and be motivated by it? Can they **authenticate** it for themselves as a useful resource for becoming aware of features of conversation and learning conversational language?

Even if we set aside the problem of whether students can authenticate the extract, the material writer is still faced with problems. The transcript has points of overlapping speech, it has unclear stretches, 'stutter-starts' (*the-the kids*), laughter, and codes which are comprehensible only to the corpus compilers (e.g., *vocal desc=*). We can 'tidy up' the transcript and re-record the voices using professional actors (as in Carter and McCarthy 1997), but, treated in that way, is it still the original text?

In one sense, tidied up and re-recorded transcripts are authentic. Like Extract 4.2, they are 'audience designed' for a specific community of users learning an L2, but in the final analysis, only learners themselves will know whether they can authenticate any text, and teachers, material writers, and publishers will ideally pay heed to learner reactions and feedback. Creating authentic material is difficult, especially for conversational speaking. McCarthy and his co-authors, in their corpus-informed spoken materials, edited corpus transcripts but always tried to retain the key language features and the flavour and flow of the original conversation. In the end, the materials were a compromise between beliefs about language, the research ethos, teachers' and learners' expectations, and publisher pressures.

Another issue is the degree to which materials reflect the local cultures of learners in ways they can relate to while at the same time recognising the international contexts in which English is likely to be used by the students. This is another delicate balance concerning authenticity that materials writers attempt to strike.

RESEARCH EVIDENCE

A study in Chile found that local EYL materials incorporated features of national geography but neglected other aspects of Chilean life. The researcher argues that materials should seek to 'bridge the gap between children's home context and the international culture where English is expected to be used' (Toledo-Sandoval 2020).

Self-study and supplementary materials are not immune from the authenticity debate. Learners around the world have benefitted from **simplified readers**, often consisting of entertaining, creative stories, which are, nonetheless, written for the purpose of language teaching and are usually based on pre-ordained, restricted vocabularies. These can be highly motivating and can provide learners with their first genuine and rewarding encounter with long texts and stories in L2, in other words, an authentic encounter with the target language.

DO THEY WORK?

The volume of EFL/ESL materials and resources has exploded in the last 30 years. Multi-level, multi-strand, multi-media courses complying with educational and cultural publishing criteria are launched amid fanfares, freebies, and catchy slogans. But do they work? How do we evaluate the success (or failure) of ELT materials?

Two approaches are apparent: **materials analysis** and **materials evaluation**. Analysis assesses what is already in the materials and is often done using a checklist of features (Littlejohn 2022). This helps in comparing materials and deciding how far they meet the needs of the curriculum. Evaluation considers what *should* be in materials and whether they achieve their stated aims and the aims of the curriculum. Establishing whether materials actually make a difference is not straightforward. Greg and Hiromi Hadley argue that approaching the end-users as subjects in a laboratory experiment is inadequate; what is required is empirical, longitudinal classroom research into the results of different materials in use (2022).

METHODOLOGY

FASHIONS COME AND GO

Different types of **methodology** (the study of systematic ways of doing things) have been fashionable or have dominated ELT over the years. In the 1960s, for example, it was widely believed that listening and oral drilling of grammar in language laboratories was the way to acquire an L2, and translation was an accepted method, a dual approach referred to as the **grammar-translation** method.

At other times, the so-called natural order guided methodology, downplaying the direct teaching of grammar. Since the 1980s, CLT has foregrounded interaction and language as 'doing'. TBL has stressed collaborative engagement with resources aimed at completing tasks. Summer (2012) provides a good summary of the evolution of methodologies.

Methodologies rest upon beliefs about language and language acquisition and exist in a close relationship with syllabuses, and as David Wilkins notes, 'inevitably it will be expected that the approach to classroom teaching will be consistent with the view of language embodied in the syllabus' (1976b: 5).

Penny Ur summarises methodologies that have been at the fore over the last 100 years, from grammar-translation to TBL and what she calls the **post-communicative approach**, whereby CLT and TBL are combined with a renewed (but meaning-focused) attention to grammar, vocabulary, and pronunciation (2012: 7–9).

WHAT LIES BEYOND?

Critiques of ELT methods (e.g., Richards and Rodgers 2001: 244–255) have led some to talk about a **postmethod** era. Decades of experience have taught us that there is no silver bullet, no one methodology for all situations (see the discussion in Thornbury 2011: 193–195). Penny Ur believes that, instead of basing ELT on a 'method', principles and procedures based on experience and the teaching situation, and knowledge and awareness of educational and linguistic research, should guide teaching (2013).

Bala Kumaravadivelu proposed a set of ten macrostrategies for teaching and says of postmethod teaching:

> it seeks to facilitate the advancement of a context-sensitive, location-specific pedagogy that is based on a true understanding of local linguistic, sociocultural, and political particularities.
>
> (2001: 544)

The macrostrategies include familiar ELT precepts such as *foster language awareness*, *contextualise linguistic input*, and *integrate language skills* (Kumaravadivelu 2003: 39–40), but they do not prescribe any method.

Crossing the threshold into the communal space occupied by teachers and learners takes us into a world where theoretical constructs take second place to capturing moment-by-moment learning opportunities. It is what you are and what you do as a teacher that matters. That is where we must go next.

NOTES

1 https://nzcurriculum.tki.org.nz/The-New-Zealand-Curriculum/ English/Learning-area-structure.
2 www.teachingenglish.org.uk/professional-development/teachers/ knowing-subject/teaching-knowledge-database/syllabus.

FURTHER READING

Graves, K. 2004. Syllabus and Curriculum Design for Second Language Teaching. In M. Celce-Murcia, D. M. Brinton and M. A. Snow (eds) *Teaching English as a Second or Foreign Language*. **Fourth edition. Boston, MA: Heinle Cengage Learning/National Geographic Leaning, 46–62.**
Kathleen Graves covers everything we discuss in this chapter and more, explaining syllabus and curriculum and tracing the evolution of different syllabus types, along with discussion of content and contexts.

Norton, J. and Buchanan, H. (eds) 2022. *The Routledge Handbook of Materials Development in Language Teaching*. **Abingdon, Oxon: Routledge.**
This book provides coverage of everything to do with materials. It includes chapters by leading experts and covers issues such as authenticity, materials for teaching skills, and materials in different learning contexts.

Summer, T. 2012. Introduction: From Method to Postmethod. In M. Eisenmann and T. Summer (eds) *Basic Issues in EFL Teaching and Learning*. **Heidelberg: Universitätsverlag Winter, 1–15.**
Theresa Summer goes into further detail than we have space for concerning the evolution of different methods in language teaching. Her survey is very clear and offers balanced critiques of the methods surveyed.

5

BEING A TEACHER

ORGANISING YOUR WORK

THE CLASSROOM

Teachers have to plan lessons, organise materials, organise students in the classroom, and think about activities and how to make the best use of interaction to facilitate learning. A plan of the classroom – seating arrangements, opportunities for pair- and group-work, ensuring students can see and hear one another, and so on – will influence participation, engagement, and learning.

PERSONAL REFLECTION

Look at the seating arrangements of three classes (Figure 5.1). Which class would you prefer to be in? What are the advantages and disadvantages of each one?

It is easier to interact with classmates when they are seated so they can see and hear one another. The physical layout will influence the kinds of interaction that can take place. Flexible arrangements enable students to work individually, in pairs, in small groups, in larger groups, or in **lockstep** (the whole class working together). However, while trying to create a student-centred environment, it is possible to make the class *too* decentralised, with students spending too much time working alone, in pairs, or in groups. The role

DOI: 10.4324/9781003350316-5

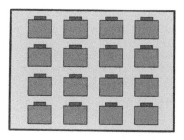
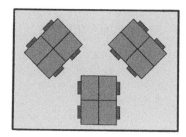
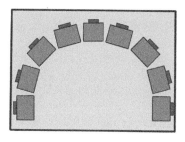

Figure 5.1 Organising the room.
Source: Image © Áine Walsh 2022.

of the teacher is crucial in maintaining a lively and engaged class where students feel valued, supported, and involved.

The best learners are those willing to take risks (Rubin 1975); teachers play an important role in establishing trust, openness, and inclusion where students feel comfortable taking risks using the L2 and in expressing their thoughts. The décor of the room can do much to foster a pleasant, relaxed atmosphere, through the use of colourful wallcharts, images, and so on.

PLANNING THE LESSON

Planning a coherent lesson, with clear **learning outcomes** (intended aims), logical teaching steps, and accurate timings is a challenge for early career teachers. Dealing with the unexpected, anticipating problems, time management, and making sure students are actively involved are key to the success of any lesson and require an ability to think on one's feet and make rapid decisions.

RESEARCH EVIDENCE

Liu's (2014) case study of a novice teacher showed how detailed lesson-planning improves confidence and helps reduce anxiety. When newly qualified teachers feel organised and prepared, students are more likely to engage and participate actively in the lesson (Nahal 2010).

Factors affecting lesson planning include the following:

- A lesson usually fits into a series; it might recycle material from a previous lesson.
- Projecting the goals that students should achieve by the end of the lesson.
- Anticipating problems students might have with language or skills (Baguley 2019).
- Balance and variety: a range of tasks and activities.
- Relative importance of different lesson stages: essential and optional elements.
- Interaction: plans for individual, pair/group, and whole class interaction; space for learning through interaction (Walsh and Li 2013).
- Tailoring to context: age, level, prior learning, interests, abilities, motivation, and so on of students, plus things like time of day and previous and next lessons.
- Post-lesson reflection. What might be changed next time? How did the plan compare with the actual lesson?

One criticism of initial teacher education courses is that they place too much emphasis on *outcomes* (lesson aims or learning outcomes). As a result, student teachers find themselves ill prepared to deal with the unexpected, make changes to their plan while teaching, identify learning opportunities, or pay sufficient attention to their relationship with students (Anderson 2015).

Lesson planning emerges most effectively from understanding the classroom context. How interactions with students influence learning, how learning is co-constructed, in other words, achieving a high level of classroom interactional competence, are all elements of the classroom context.

A context-based approach (Bax 2003) sees context as a microcosm which can be studied and understood in great detail. Central to context-based teaching is a focus on interaction, developing what Leo Van Lier calls an *ecological* approach to language learning, 'that focuses primarily on the quality of learning opportunities, of classroom interaction and of educational experience in general' (2010: 2). In the natural world, any change to the ecology, even relatively small ones, will have consequences elsewhere. The same is true of the language classroom, for example, introducing a new test, changing the coursebook, placing more emphasis on speaking, or using new technology. Furthermore, the ecology of the classroom is influenced and continuously reshaped by the many different energies, personalities, individual quirks, and behaviours of everyone involved, which can often present as different strands competing for the teacher's (and everyone's) attention. Figure 5.2 takes a tongue-in-cheek look at the labels we as teachers often attach to individuals in our classes. However, we should constantly remind ourselves that learners are unique human beings who behave differently at different times and how easy but unwise it can be to

Figure 5.2 Difficult learners.
Source: Image © Áine Walsh 2022.

fall back on generalisations and stereotypes when faced with 'difficult' learners.

Classroom management (CM) is concerned with the strategies teachers use to create a comfortable, purposeful learning environment. Heather Buchanan and Ivor Timmis set out to research how CM is regarded by practising teachers and teacher trainers (2019). Their survey focused on pre-service and in-service teacher education programmes and looked at what skills or strategies were associated with CM and which ones could be trained. The top five rated skills/techniques were (a) setting up group and pair work, (b) monitoring activities effectively, (c) maintaining discipline, (d) establishing rapport, and (e) making on-the-spot decisions in response to classroom events. However, (c) and (e) scored low on trainability.

YOU AND YOUR COLLEAGUES

NATIVE AND EXPERT USERS

Current estimates indicate that there are three times as many non-native speakers (NNSs) of English as native speakers (NSs). Of 1,453 million users of English, 373 million are NSs (those who speak English as their first language) and 1,080 million are NNSs (those who speak English as their second language).[1]

One consequence of the rapid rise of English as a world language has been the proliferation of NNS teachers of EFL/ESL. According to Freeman et al. (2015), non-native English-speaking teachers (NNESTs) make up 80% of English teachers worldwide. Put simply, of the 15 million teachers of English in the world, 12 million are NNESTs. However, binary distinctions such as NS/NNS and NEST/NNEST are problematic and have led to many debates and dilemmas about what it means to be 'native' or 'non-native' (Canagarajah 1999). NS teachers are sometimes regarded as being 'better', 'more competent', using more 'natural' language, and so on and may be seen as the go-to person in the school staffroom when language questions crop up. Such thinking has had an influence on many aspects of ELT, including materials, methods, assessment, teacher education, policy and planning, and hiring practices (see, for example, Leung 2005; Llurda 2016). Yet it is worth noting that, over the decades, some of the most important and influential accounts of English grammar have been authored by NNS scholars from Scandinavia and the Netherlands. The NNS perspective on the L2 is often keener and more objective than that of the NS.

To safeguard the interests of NNESTs, a professional movement has been established, known as the NNEST movement (Braine 2018). The movement 'acknowledges, supports and promotes ethnic, racial, cultural, religious, gender and linguistic diversity in TESOL' (Selvi 2019: 187).

OBSERVATION

There are four principal reasons for observing a class: training, professional development, assessment, and management. In the context of professional development, observation is either done by a colleague, a peer, a critical friend, or teachers observing their own teaching. Observing other teachers and being observed are sensitive practices which require trust and respect; the aim of observation is to shed light on an existing issue, to explore different approaches, or to develop better understandings of classroom practice.

Mutually agreed-upon observation – observing a colleague and having the colleague observe you – is one approach. Classrooms are complex environments: so much goes on at any one time, it would be impossible to capture everything. It is difficult to make good-quality recordings; it is also extremely laborious and time consuming to transcribe a whole lesson. Instead, 'snapshot recordings', three-to-four-minute video-clips (not transcribed) can provide plenty of material for discussion and reflection. These can be made at different stages of a lesson. Viewing recordings and discussing them with a colleague can be a fruitful way of gaining new understandings and exploring alternative ways of conducting activities.

Self-observation is another approach. The SETT framework (Self Evaluation of Teacher Talk) is an example of a tool which could be used to analyse a recording. It is presented in full in Chapter 6 and exemplified further in Chapter 8.

YOU AND YOUR STUDENTS

THE HUMAN FACTOR

For all the research cited and guidelines provided in this book, there are things teachers have little control over, such as mixed abilities in the same class, the attitudes of individuals, their liking or disliking you, the ups and downs of their attention, occasional acts of indiscipline, differing physical and mental abilities, and so on.

Motivation, what drives a learner, is a significant factor. One scholar lists three key elements of motivation: willingness to put effort into learning, goal orientation, and a feeling of enjoyment (Gardner 2001). Motivation in EFL/ESL can spring from different sources. Some learners wish to identify with an English-speaking community and aim to achieve a high level of proficiency to integrate in that community. Elena (see Chapter 3), a refugee, wishes to become a fully participating member of UK society; her motivation is **integrative**. She also knows that, realistically, a good level of English will give her better career chances and earning potential than if she were a struggling beginner, so part of her motivation is **instrumental**. Other learners may have instrumental goals as their main or sole motivation. Motivation is non-linear (it does not develop in a straight line), it may go up and down or back and forth and may be influenced by different contextual factors. There may be occasional 'surges' in motivation related to long-term goals (Dörnyei et al. 2016). One work on motivation lists, among other factors, learning strategies, learner autonomy, and the learning task – all of which can affect a learner's motivation (Dörnyei and Schmidt 2001). The teacher's personal motivation can also play a role (Dewaele 2020).

Mixed classes where high achievers sit alongside lower achievers can dull the motivation of students at either end of the scale. Student performance may also be influenced by shyness, fear of making mistakes, boredom, tiredness, and so on. Not all learners are equally abled. Issues such as dyslexia, mobility problems, visual or auditory impairment, stuttering and stammering, mental wellbeing, and learning difficulties all require empathy and individual attention. Fortunately, there is plentiful advice in the published literature to guide teachers through such challenging situations (e.g., Domagala-Zyék and Kontra 2016; Kormos 2020; Daloiso 2017). The challenges for such students may be greater, but their motivation may be as high or higher than that of normally abled students.

INTELLIGENCE

The theory of **multiple intelligences** (**MIs**) was developed by the psychologist Howard Gardner (see Torff and Gardner 1999 for a summary). It claims that different types of intelligence exist rather than 'intelligence' as one undifferentiated human capacity. As mentioned in Chapter 3, some people are more naturally inclined towards visual or kinaesthetic learning, while others are more cognitively oriented. Similar variations can be seen in intelligence: Gardner lists eight variations. MI theory has influenced approaches to ELT but has not been without its critics, especially owing to its lack of experimental evidence (White 2006). Looking at the strategies learners apply to particular tasks and situations may be a more fruitful way of understanding individual learners and different approaches to learning (Klein 1997). The challenge is not to lump all learners into one category but to offer teaching that appeals to individual approaches to learning, mixing and matching a variety of activity types.

POWER, ROLES, RELATIONSHIPS

Even in the most collaborative classroom, it is the teacher who has the power and responsibility to see that the lesson starts and finishes and moves efficiently towards its goals. This is a powerful role, but the teacher–learner relationship is not just an academic or managerial one; it is also a social–emotional one.

PERSONAL REFLECTION

Think of your schooldays and different teachers you had. How was the balance between the academic relationship (effective teaching, subject interest, etc.) and the social/personal side (distance, friendship, strictness, etc.)?

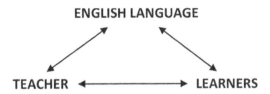

Figure 5.3 The EFL/ESL communication triangle.

Power also suggests the teacher has control over the subject matter and that it is the teacher's job to 'deliver' the subject matter to the students. However, theories of communication paint a dynamic picture of the relationship between the speaker, the listener, and the subject matter, with all three shaping the communication. This **dialogic** view of language comes from the work of Mikhail Bakhtin (1981). Put simply, the teacher does not just channel English to the students; they too shape the process both vis-à-vis the teacher and vis-à-vis the language. The channels always face both ways, in constant dialogue (Figure 5.3).

In Figure 5.3, all three participants in the learning process exercise mutual influence. The subject-matter (in this case the English language) is not a powerless presence; it influences the thinking, behaviour, and emotions of the other participants. While the teacher undoubtedly has powers with regard to the organisation and progress of the lesson, these powers are incidental to the job of shaping communication with the learners to explore learning opportunities in the subject matter.

However, Penny Ur injects a note of realism into what seems to be an attractive theory of communication for the ELT classroom. She discusses the role of the teacher as a **facilitator** (someone who supports and eases learning) rather than a dictator but notes that the complexities of the L2 are something learners can hardly be expected to discover for themselves:

> Effective language teaching, therefore, should arguably be based on a substantial amount of teacher-initiated instruction; though student-centred activation has an essential place as well.

(Ur 2012: 16)

The basic shape of the communication triangle remains, but it is tempered by the teacher's responsibilities.

The first day of a new class is filled with anticipation, nervousness, and degrees of anxiety. Ideally, everyone hopes to get off on the right foot; first impressions, rightly or wrongly, influence things further down the line. Here again, the power to create success or to fuel failure is a joint, dialogic activity but with the teacher bearing central responsibility. The British Council's *Teaching English* website provides a selection of icebreakers for that vital first encounter.[2]

The social/emotional relationship can also be influenced by class size: the larger the class, the more difficult it is to create personal relationships. Jim Scrivener notes that eye contact becomes complicated in large classes (Scrivener 2011: 331). Conversely, the one-to-one lesson can involve intense, positive personal relations, but tiredness, boredom, or external factors on either side can cause problems (see the discussion in Harmer 2007: 122–123).

RESEARCH EVIDENCE

Research into one-to-one teaching shows that success is influenced by the way the teacher behaves and the strategies they adopt. Positive feedback is important when the learner is heading on the right path towards solving a problem and in keeping the learner on the right path while still encouraging them to work towards solving the problem. Another strategy is blaming the task rather than the student when things are perceived as difficult (Merrill et al. 1995).

Whether whole-group or one-to-one, the teacher-student relationship will evolve, and, if handled well, warmth, trust, security, mutual respect, enjoyment, and a feeling of progress will grow and feed into pleasurable learning. Recently, attention has turned towards **social-emotional learning**, which stresses learning a language to not only function in social or professional contexts but also as emotion-centred human beings. TESOL International provides a guide to social-emotional learning and creating positive relationships in a collaborative environment (Zacarian 2021).

IDENTITIES

You are the teacher. They are the students. These simple statements conceal the complexity of personal **identity**. We also know if we are someone's sibling, parent, child, friend, colleague, customer, mentor, team-mate, housemate, patient, neighbour. We have multiple identities that come into play at different times (Figure 5.4).

Different aspects of identity become relevant at different moments. Yet, as teachers, we naturally see a group or class as a collective identity to which the individual students belong; likewise, they may think of 'the teachers' as a collective body. People coalesce into *in-groups* and *out-groups*. Bethan Benwell and Elizabeth Stokoe explain things thus:

> Put simply, the ingroup is the one to which an individual 'belongs' and the 'outgroup' is seen as 'outside' and different from this group.
>
> (2006: 25)

Benwell and Stokoe demonstrate how identity is created and maintained through discourse. The challenge to teachers is to create,

Figure 5.4 Multiple identities.
Source: Image © Áine Walsh 2022.

through appropriate interaction, a sense of in-group identity in class, where nobody feels alienated and no individual is considered an outsider. This is easier said than done and may involve acceptance of fluidity, eccentricity, and individuals' inscrutability. Learners with different interests and aspirations, different genders, ethnicities, abilities, disabilities, religions, and cultures – all fall within the purview of the teacher's task of creating a socially cohesive group. Despite the paradigm of the class as a *community*, experienced teachers will confess that sometimes groups inexplicably gel and other times they don't. For the teacher, navigating identities within the class is as great a responsibility as effective teaching of language and skills.

RESEARCH EVIDENCE

Bonny Norton says, 'Research on identity suggests that the extent to which a learner speaks or is silent, and writes, reads, or resists has much to do with the extent to which the learner is valued in any given institution or community' (2011: 326).

WE ARE WHAT WE SAY

How learners experience and use language in the classroom builds their identity as members of the classroom community. This notion is reflected in debates on **translanguaging**. Translanguaging occurs when speakers draw on their repertoire of whatever language(s) they know, going from one to another in moment-by-moment strategic decisions to facilitate communication. The term **code switching** (changing from one language to another mid-stream) and translanguaging are seen by scholars as two different things. Code switching tends to occur predictably and at certain places in a bilingual speaker's use of their two languages. Li Wei explains translanguaging in a blog which examines the two different terms:

> Translanguaging defines language as a multilingual, multimodal, and multisensory sense- and meaning-making resource.
>
> (https://blog.oup.com/2018/05/translanguaging-code-switching-difference/)

The teacher may be unsure how to react if learners unexpectedly have recourse to their L1 in class. They may do this when answering questions or carrying out tasks in pairs and groups, or just chatting surreptitiously with one another. One may feel duty bound to say, 'English only, please!' because we generally believe that maximum use of the target language by everyone is best practice. And the teacher may ponder if they are doing the right thing in using the learners' L1 to explain grammar, as a shortcut to the meanings of words, or to call the class to order. This happens often in situations where all the students share an L1. Translation-explanations are themselves examples of translanguaging.

PERSONAL REFLECTION

Think of your schooldays or any experience of learning a foreign language. How much did the teacher use L2 and how much did they use your L1? What difference do you think it made?

Rather than see a learner's use of different languages as a sign of a lack of competence, advocates of translanguaging see it as a positive aspect of engagement with L2 and as a feature of the learner's emergent identity as a bilingual or multilingual individual rather than as a 'failed native speaker' (see Chapter 3).

The teacher retains the ultimate authority and responsibility to manage a coherent class while creating a cohesive community in which everyone feels involved and is making progress in English. In classes of mixed language backgrounds, interventions by students in languages other than English may generate frustration and impatience. On the other hand, in one-to-one lessons, teacher and learner may help each other through translanguaging.

Translanguaging is a strategy whereby emergent multilingual identities are made plain. Its theoretical foundation is **plurilingualism**, the idea that teachers and learners can fully exploit their knowledge of languages and intercultural awareness. The CEFR's founding body, the Council of Europe, explains the meaning of plurilingualism in relation to language education, which:

is no longer seen as simply to achieve 'mastery' of one or two, or even three languages, each taken in isolation, with the 'ideal native speaker' as the ultimate model. Instead, the aim is to develop a linguistic repertory, in which all linguistic abilities have a place.

(2001: 5)

JUST YOU AND ME

One-to-one lessons are a special type of learning environment. In chapter 3, we saw Elena, a refugee living in the United Kingdom, sitting with her volunteer teacher (Figure 3.2 on p. 61). They work together for an hour several times a week by mutual arrangement. After almost a year together, they have become friends. The social aspect of their relationship is important: Elena often brings small gifts of food she has prepared, and the teacher often advises Elena on non-linguistic matters of settling into UK life. Both occasionally feel tired after a day's work and frustration over difficulties of explaining or understanding the forms and meanings of English (Elena's teacher: personal correspondence).

INFORMATION ADD-ON

We asked Elena's teacher to comment on their one-to-one lessons:
'It's very rewarding – you can see immediate progress, and because you only have to focus on one person's learning problems, it seems more efficient and effective.
'It can be very intense and intensive, and tiring for both parties. The learner has no "pause button" and is constantly being asked to do something and the teacher can't set up pair or group work with others to change their role.'

(Reproduced by kind permission)

Tasha Bleistein and Marilyn Lewis look at the social relationship in one-to-one teaching and the question of role boundaries, how close teacher and student should become, and whether any developing social relationship should be clearly demarcated as separate from the professional relationship (2015: 43–44). Another issue is the extent to which the student continues to depend on the teacher's input or whether the one-to-one situation can foster learner autonomy to the same or a greater extent as in learner-centred activities with groups. Bleistein and Lewis say:

> The most basic way to build autonomy is to ask learners what will help to make them successful. Simple choices throughout a tutoring session can build this skill.
>
> (2015: 56)

This approach can also contribute to a student's emergent identity as an agent of their own language learning.

DOING LANGUAGE TEACHING

SO FAR

Chapter 1 was about the raw material of ELT, the English language. Chapter 2 looked at the skills and how they interacted. Chapter 3 looked at learners and language acquisition, and Chapter 4 looked at syllabuses and methods.

But none of that looked closely at what you, the teacher, can do in class with your learners. We turn now to some questions around teaching *language*. We will not direct you how to behave once you close the classroom door; that you will decide as a responsible adult who has the basics under their belt and guides are available to help with the practical aspects of teaching the forms of English (e.g. Thornbury 1999, 2002; Kelly 2000).

PPP? III? TBL? PLEASE NOTICE

One decision the teacher has to make is how to exploit teaching material. Globally published language courses often make this decision for you, with teacher's manuals laboriously instructing the teacher in what to do and say at every moment of the teaching sequence. However, there are radically different ways of showing and explaining what you want your learners to learn and use and helping them to get there.

Figure 5.5 PPP: presentation.
Source: Image © Áine Walsh 2022.

The technique called **PPP (presentation–practice–production)** has held sway for many decades and is probably the most widely used teaching sequence. The teacher might show the class a picture or play an audio/video clip to demonstrate a target language feature. Figure 5.5 shows various people and things in different places. The focus is the prepositions *in*, *on*, and *at* and the differences between them. The teacher explains each picture, probably carefully stressing the target words (*the man is standing **at** the bus stop, the women are talking **in** the kitchen*, etc.). This is the first P, *presentation*, the setting of the context and flagging up of the target language.

The teacher next sets up *practice*, maybe an informal drill, asking questions such as *Where are the cups in picture 1? And the two people in picture 3?* or else a gap-fill exercise. The procedure will be repeated until the desired patterns are used fluently and accurately. During the final P, *production*, learners can direct people, move objects to different positions in the class, and ask one another questions (*Where are your books? They're on the table/on my desk. Where is Teresa? Standing at the window/at the door*).

PPP has been used worldwide for decades, and it works for the drilling of grammar, vocabulary, and pronunciation. We authors have used it at one time or another in our teaching. But no technique is a silver bullet, and PPP is best used mixed with other approaches. PPP has had its critics (see Sato 2010). Jeremy Harmer says that it 'seems to assume that students learn "in straight lines" – that is, starting from no knowledge, through highly restricted sentence-based utterances and on to immediate production' (2007: 66). Harmer presents an alternative: ESA (*engage, study, activate*). He claims ESA is flexible, not a fixed sequence (2007: 66–68).

PPP is best suited to lower proficiency levels where clear, unambiguous presentations of basic structures, pronunciation, and vocabulary enable learners to engage with material, practise in controlled sessions, and acquire basic knowledge relatively quickly. More advanced learners typically benefit from more cognitively demanding approaches, skill integration, and greater complexity of spoken and written input and output in the classroom.

PPP and its emphasis on drill-type practice has mostly been compared unfavourably with task-based learning (TBL), with its focus on meaning and the integration of skills. But TBL too has come under scrutiny. Michael Swan criticises claims of the superiority of TBL over other approaches as 'legislation by hypothesis', in other words a claim made without proper evidence of its effectiveness (2005). Mixing and matching PPP and TBL may be a more sensible route to effective learning outcomes.

PERSONAL REFLECTION

If you learnt a second language in a formal setting, did the teacher use PPP, or was it more like TBL, or something different?

Ronald Carter and Michael McCarthy developed an alternative to PPP, which they referred to as **the three Is** (1995). Their research into spoken grammar raised a number of questions with regard to practical teaching and the use of PPP, such as, 'How does one "present" transaction boundaries? How does one "produce" discourse markers naturally?' (McCarthy 1998: 67). They proposed instead a sequence based around language awareness and working out the form-meaning relation through observation of texts and interaction with the teacher and classmates. These were the three stages:

Illustration

The target language is presented in short texts/audio clips in natural contexts.

Interaction

As with the triangle on p. 132, there is three-way interaction between the material, the teachers, and the learners, focusing on the form-meaning relationship.

Induction

From separate instances of the form-meaning relationship and via scaffolded interaction, learners induce the meaning or grammatical convention.

(McCarthy 1998: 67–68)

McCarthy and McCarten (2018) offer further detail on the three stages. After these three steps, the lesson can move from controlled practice to freer and personalised production.

The three Is depend on language awareness and noticing. **Language awareness** has long been discussed as a central element of purposeful learning (see Essen 2008 for a historical overview). Building awareness may mean adjusting learners' expectations as to what can fruitfully be learnt about the L2. Many learners come to class expecting a diet of grammar rules, vocabulary, and pronunciation, with the four skills bolted on top. Discourse skills and strategies, our notion of the 'fifth skill', for example, may be alien to them, but the teacher can help learners to become language aware, perhaps by pointing out similar phenomena in the learners' L1(s). All human languages use their formal resources in the service of creating and maintaining interaction at the level of pragmatics and discourse, and this can be exploited in a non-jargonistic way in the classroom.

To engage fully with the language, to participate in classroom interaction in collaborative and scaffolded learning, requires the skill of **noticing** L2 forms and how they operate in context. **Noticing** has been extensively researched, and a distinction is often drawn between **incidental** learning, for example, picking up vocabulary during extensive reading, and **intentional** learning, where the learner focuses on either the material at hand or particular L2 targets. Engaging with the material and noticing interesting linguistic features in it may pay off in some incidental learning, but true noticing involves a focus on the form-meaning relationship of particular items. As Richard Schmidt puts it:

> what must be attended to and noticed is not just the input in a global sense but whatever features of the input are relevant for the target system . . . that is to say, in order to acquire phonology one must attend to phonology; in order to acquire pragmatics, one must notice both linguistic forms and the relevant contextual features.

(1993: 209)

Schmidt reflected on his own learning of Portuguese and showed that what he 'noticed' in the input correlated with what he had learnt, from the evidence of recordings of his interactions with native speakers (1990). This was an endorsement of the value of noticing in learning and one which underpins the three Is. Examples of activities to encourage noticing can be found in the multi-level materials produced by McCarthy et al. (2005, 2012, 2014a and b) and in an article on the role of practice by McCarthy and McCarten (2018).

The teaching sequences suggested by PPP, ESA, and the three Is all have their place in ELT, and the practical teacher will adapt materials and techniques to particular contexts and changing situations in class.

ERROR CORRECTION

Whether and how learners' errors should be corrected has long been a subject of debate in ELT. In Chapter 3, we saw how the concept of interlanguage changed perceptions as to the place of errors in language development, while translanguaging suggests that exploiting L1 and, in the process, transferring an L1 form inappropriately into L2, does not necessarily have to be viewed negatively.

Error correction is a complex matter, and best practice responds to moment-by-moment context rather than theory or orthodoxy. Many students like to be corrected and feel they are being short-changed if correction is not forthcoming; others are less bothered by the absence of correction. Context includes considering the type of activity being undertaken and how it relates to the fluency-accuracy-complexity triangle. Fluency-oriented activities can be hindered if the teacher constantly corrects formal errors; on the other hand, accuracy-oriented activities are the place for discussing the significance or otherwise of errors.

Many scholars prefer the term *feedback* to *error correction*. More specifically, tying in with SCT, the idea of **scaffolded feedback** involves the teacher discussing the error with the learner, urging them towards self-correction (Rassaei 2014). Brinton (2014) lists different ways the teacher can approach learner errors (see also Bohlke 2014).

RESEARCH EVIDENCE

Penny Ur carried out a survey of learners' attitudes to being corrected. Her results show that the great majority want to be corrected and prefer to be told what the mistake was and the correct form rather than having to work it out themselves (Ur 2012: 91–94).

There can be no doubt that certain formal errors (defined as departures from the conventions of the variety of L2 being learnt) can be attributed to the learner's L1. For example, speakers of languages which have no article system comparable to that of standard British (BrE) and American English (AmE), such as Chinese languages, tend to have problems using the BrE/AmE definite and indefinite articles. Swan and Smith (2001) list predictable departures from standard BrE grammatical, lexical, and phonological conventions in the interlanguage of learners representing a wide variety of first languages.

GRAMMAR IN THE CLASSROOM

SIMPLICITY TO COMPLEXITY

In modern coursebooks, the grammar syllabus is typically graded to take learners from simpler and more common structures and items (e.g. simple present tense, pronouns, prepositions) via more complex features such as present perfect and various forms relating to future time (*will, going to, be to*, etc.), all the way to low-frequency complex structures such as the future perfect (*I will have been working . . .*). When Michael McCarthy looked at some popular coursebooks and their grammar syllabuses, he noted a general consensus as to what should be taught, which we referred to as the *ELT canon* in Chapter 4. This was particularly true at beginner and lower proficiency levels. However, as syllabuses moved towards the advanced level, there was less of a consensus and considerable variation. This posed the question as to when and how one should introduce complex structures such as future perfect forms. McCarthy's conclusion was that corpus research was needed to give teachers and material writers guidance for advanced-level grammar teaching (2013, 2015, 2016a). Grammar teaching covers a wide range of form, meaning, and function, and accuracy, fluency, and semantic and pragmatic complexity increase as the learner moves up the proficiency levels (O'Keeffe and Mark 2017).

POWER OF THE -ING FORM

In this book, we refer not to *rules* but to grammar *conventions*, since *rule* suggests an imposition by people or institutions in authority. Grammar is not like that, nor does it necessarily help to just teach learners rules. The applied linguist Diane Larsen-Freeman rejects a rule-bound notion of grammar as a hard-wired mental competence. She prefers the approach that sees grammar as *doing* things socially with language, what she calls *grammaring* (Larsen-Freeman 2003: ch.4), exploiting the dynamic meaning of the *-ing* form in English. *Grammaring* implies grammar is best learnt in contexts rather than through slot-and-fill sentences and best seen as a dynamic resource. Spoken and written discourses are where the conventions of grammar are best seen doing their work creating meaning and interaction rather than demonstrating 'rules'.

Although grammar may be effectively displayed in charts and tables in coursebooks, repeated experience of input and output, trying as best we can to foster usage-based acquisition (see Chapter 3), may lead to deeper learning and automaticity. Automaticity is an element of fluency in the fluency-accuracy-complexity triangle.

Further considerations in teaching grammar include:

- Is the target written grammar, spoken grammar, or just a general subject called *grammar*? Studies of spoken grammar have shown its special characteristics (Carter and McCarthy 2017).
- If the focus is on spoken grammar, what variety of English becomes the model (e.g., South African, Indian, Irish)? Spoken grammar is more likely to reflect local variation (Farrell 2020).

VOCABULARY: IN THE MIND AND IN USE

GETTING TO THE CORE

Although grammar is important, vocabulary is indisputably the biggest single element in learning an L2. Corpora such as the BNC and American National Corpus (ANC) show tens of thousands of words in circulation in present-day English. But in everyday use, especially spoken language, speakers can get by with as few as 3,000 words. There are also chunks and other word combinations of various kinds, as we saw in Chapter 1. The core vocabulary of around 3,000 words plus high-frequency chunks reflects the fact that these items work overtime, while the rest of the vocabulary is infrequent.

RESEARCH EVIDENCE

McCarthy (2023: 25) shows that the 4,000 most frequent words in the Spoken BNC 2014 account for around 90% of all the words used by the speakers in that corpus. Other research suggests that the first 3,000 most frequent words in corpora represent the core, high-frequency vocabulary (Nation and Waring 1997; Schmitt and Schmitt 2014; Szudarski 2018).

REALISTIC GOALS

The first 3,000–4,000 words give a good return for learners, but 3,000 words is still a daunting target. Much depends on whether the target is **receptive** vocabulary (words you store and can understand) or **productive** (words you can quickly access and use).

Receptive vocabulary is always the bigger for native and non-native users. Receptive vocabulary can be built incidentally or intentionally through reading and listening. Productive vocabulary requires repetition and reinforcement and the development of automaticity.

Paul Nation and Robert Waring advocate learning the core vocabulary as quickly as possible, which may involve, in the initial stages, learning from cards with words written on them, which may seem an old-fashioned approach (1997). However, if it works, it should not be rejected on grounds of fashion or orthodoxy. Nation also argues that, once the core has been tackled, a more useful approach is to help learners develop autonomy through vocabulary learning strategies, so they can tackle the thousands of low-frequency words which they will bump into after they have left the teacher's hands (1990; see also Schmitt 1997).

Another aspect of vocabulary development is the distinction between **vocabulary breadth** (how many words you know) and **vocabulary depth** (what you know about those words). When you meet a new L2 word, you encounter its spelling and/or its pronunciation. You may work out its grammatical class and guess or infer its meaning. On successive encounters with the word, you may learn further properties: collocations, use in compounds and idioms, level of formality/informality, connotations, and so on. In this way, breadth does not increase, but depth does.

Some words are more difficult to learn than others. Batia Laufer lists reasons a word might be easy or difficult, involving factors such as pronounceability, morphological complexity, and so on (1997). Recycling vocabulary, offering a dozen or so encounters with the same item over time, repetition and reinforcement of meaning and use are effective techniques to embed new items.

ALL IN THE MIND

Vocabulary is stored in memory; the 'storehouse' is a feature of the human brain, referred to as the **mental lexicon**. The brain is a delicate network, an unimaginably entangled multitude of circuits firing charges from one to another, creating traces in memory of different strengths. New words seek their home somewhere in the network, in sense relationships with other words based on all the types outlined in Chapter 1.

For a new word to find its most productive place in the mental lexicon (*place* is just a metaphor for the invisible, dynamic network), it must be learnt in depth. Depth of knowledge is something that develops over time; a beginner's L2 mental lexicon may manifest weaker network connections than an advanced learner's, which benefits from having seen words many times and building up complex profiles and interrelations.

Brent Wolter suggests that the learner's L2 mental lexicon is not fundamentally different from the native speaker's (2001); both lexicons evolve and forge new networks over time and never reach a static, permanent state. In short, there is a direct parallel between teaching depth of vocabulary knowledge and a complex, automatically and accurately accessible mental lexicon. It is not just how many words you know; what matters is how they all relate to one another in the mental lexicon.

PRONUNCIATION

WHOSE PRONUNCIATION?

Pronunciation teaching is an example of how the pendulum swings in fashions and methods in ELT. Once a central element in language teaching, pronunciation lost its importance when communicative teaching (CLT) and its emphasis on meaning rather than form swept in during the 1980s. Of late, pronunciation has made a comeback, especially since English has become a global resource.

The first choice is what model to teach. Decades ago, the standard model of **received pronunciation** (RP; the pronunciation of the upper echelons of society) dominated British-oriented EFL. Over time, North American English grew in global influence such that major EFL courses are often divided between those for British (BrE) markets and those for American English (AmE). The growth of World Englishes and English as a lingua franca have led to a rethinking of pronunciation teaching, with greater acceptance of different dialects and varieties in how sounds are articulated and a focus on **intelligibility** (understandable communication) in situated discourse (Seidlhofer 2001; Derwing and Munro 2005).

Intelligibility involves audience design (see Chapter 2): good speakers construct their talk with their interlocutors in mind, including how they pronounce words, regardless of the chosen variety of the language in question. That is not to say that learners have to aspire to native-speaker pronunciation. One's accent, whether native or non-native, is part of one's identity.

INTONATION PLUS PRONUNCIATION

Teachers often give learners practise in articulating English phonemes, but it is only in situated discourse that intelligibility can be judged. A major component of spoken discourse is intonation, the rise and fall of the voice as the spoken message is articulated (see Chapter 1).

Once the repertoire of phonemes has been practised, practice in stress patterns and the basic tones of intonation can help with overall intelligibility and offers the opportunity of mixing a top-down focus on intonation and a bottom-up focus on pronunciation to achieve overall intelligibility. Comprehension happens in context, at the discourse level, and problematic individual words and sounds from the listener's point of view are often resolved in context.

CONCLUSION

This chapter has ranged far and wide, since it lays out the basics of what the teacher has to tackle as a professional – roles, relationships, and responsibilities; understanding students; and decisions relating to teaching the language. But it is in the moment-by-moment activity in the classroom where we really see ELT in action, and so it is to the classroom and what teachers and learners say and do there that we turn next.

NOTES

1 www.ethnologue.com/language/eng/.
2 www.teachingenglish.org.uk/professional-development/teachers/knowing-subject/d-h/ice-breakers.

FURTHER READING

Brinton, D. 2014. Tools and techniques of effective second/foreign language teaching. In M. Celce-Murcia, D. M. Brinton and M. A. Snow (eds) *Teaching English as a Second or Foreign Language*. Fourth

edition. Boston, MA: Heinle Cengage Learning/National Geographic Leaning, 340–361.
This is an excellent follow-up to many of themes dealt with in this chapter, including methods of presentation, student grouping, teacher discourse, and error correction, all in an accessible style with practical tips for the classroom.

Dörnyei, Z., Henry, A. and Muir, C. 2016. Motivational Currents in Language Learning. Abingdon, Oxon: Routledge.
Zoltan Dörnyei's works on motivation are unsurpassed, and this one looks at motivation over the long term and analyses the personal/emotional features of motivation. It goes much further in detail and into new territory than our chapter is able to.

Kelly, G. 2000. *How to Teach Pronunciation*. Harlow: Longman.

Thornbury, S. 1999. *How to Teach Grammar*. Harlow: Longman.

Thornbury, S. 2002. *How to Teach Vocabulary*. Harlow: Longman.
This series of *How to* . . . books provides detailed guidelines, tips, and practical examples of teaching the basics of the formal aspects of English. The authors are experienced teachers and teacher educators, and the books are designed to increase both knowledge and skills for teachers.

Ur, P. 2012. *A Course in English Language Teaching*. Second edition. Cambridge: Cambridge University Press.
Chapter 19 of Penny Ur's book is particularly helpful on learner differences in mixed classes, including different personalities, learning styles, motivation, and attitudes, and teaching high and low achievers.

6

CLASSROOM INTERACTION

INTERACTING

In any classroom, interaction is central to teaching and learning. Classroom interaction is rapid, involves a number of people, and is constantly shifting as a lesson develops and topics and thoughts arise and recede (Figure 6.1).

Classroom interaction also has many elements; one utterance might perform several functions at the same time. Consider, for example, a simple question asked by a teacher: 'What time does this class end?' Depending on the context and how this question is asked, it could be a request for information, encouragement to complete a task, a test of how to tell the time in English, an admonishment of a student arriving late, and so on.

It is probably true to say that any efforts to improve the teaching and learning process should begin with a focus on **classroom interaction**. It is through language and interaction that learning takes place; all aspects of classroom life depend on the quality of language in interaction: acquiring new knowledge, developing skills, establishing relationships, providing and receiving feedback – the list goes on. Put simply, classroom interaction is where the action is. In an ELT classroom, language is both the goal and the means of achieving that goal: 'the vehicle and object of study' (Long 1983: 134). For English language teachers, there is a need to understand both the language we are teaching and the language we are using *for* teaching.

Our goal as language teachers, then, is to develop a closer understanding of communication in the classroom. The way we use

DOI: 10.4324/9781003350316-6

Figure 6.1 Interaction: where the action is.
Source: Image © Áine Walsh 2023.

language to promote interaction underpins all classroom activity, including managing groups and materials, organising tasks and activities, giving instructions, eliciting responses, and providing feedback. According to Van Lier (1988: 87), 'interaction is the most important thing on the curriculum'. Interaction is emergent in the dialogic triangle (Chapter 5, p. 104), where teacher, students, and subject matter all participate.

TALKING THE TALK

There are four key features of classroom interaction: control of the interaction, speech modification, elicitation (asking questions), and repair (error correction). These four features are the most likely to influence learning; they are also found in any language classroom the world over.

Teachers control classroom interaction because roles are unequal; they are *asymmetrical* as teachers are in a position of power or authority. Teachers have the final control of the patterns of communication that occur and can direct and manage the interaction. Even in the most learner-centred classroom, teachers decide who speaks, when, to whom, and for how long. Teachers interrupt when they like, take the floor, hand over a turn, direct the discussion, and switch topics. As Michael Breen puts it, it is the teacher who 'orchestrates the interaction' (1998: 119). Although there will be times when learners participate more actively, they typically take their cues from the teacher, responding to questions, carrying out instructions, listening, and generally playing a more passive role in the interaction.

If we look at an extract from an ELT classroom, we see quite clearly how teachers control the interaction. In Extract 6.1, a group of multilingual, intermediate adult EFL students are discussing issues about law and order in their respective countries.

EXTRACT 6.1

T: ok Erica could you explain something about law and order in Japan what happens if you commit a crime?

L1: almost same as Britain policeman come to take somebody to police station

T: yes

L1: and prisoner questioned and if he is (*5 seconds unintelligible*)

T: yes what's the verb Eric Erica . . . if she or he yes commits a crime they go to

L1: they go to court yes but if they he they didn't do that they can go home

T: they can go home very good indeed right what happens in Brazil?

(Walsh 2006)

In Extract 6.1, the teacher (T) controls the discourse in several ways. She selects who may talk (line 1), controls the topic of conversation (l.2), evaluates the learner's performance (l. 8), and manages both language form (*what's the verb* in l.6) and the message (*they go home* in l.8). In l.9, the teacher addresses another student by asking another question (*what happens in Brazil*). Throughout this extract, turns are managed, participation is limited, and students take all their cues from the teacher.

Another feature of Extract 6.1 is that it follows a very specific structure, incorporating a question, an answer, and an evaluation. This three-part exchange structure, the initiation, response, feedback (IRF) (Initiation, Response, Feedback) sequence outlined in Chapter 1, is a basic building block of classroom interaction. For every response made by a learner, the teacher makes two: initiation (asking a question, for example) and feedback (reacting to a student's contribution). This, in part, at least, explains why the amount of teacher talk in a classroom is considerably greater than student talk.

Breen's (1998) metaphor of the teacher 'orchestrating the discourse' is very much in evidence throughout Extract 6.1. It is a teacher's ability to control who may participate, direct student contributions, and manage both topic and language that create or restrict opportunities for learning (Walsh 2002). As we shall see later in this chapter, teachers may create 'space for learning' (Walsh and Li 2013) as much through their choice of language and management of interaction as through their ability to use appropriate materials or methods.

Teachers, through their unique status in a classroom and by their power and authority, control content, procedure, and participation. Teachers also ask a lot of questions, the second feature of classroom interaction: elicitation. Elicitation techniques are simply the ways in which teachers get students to respond. Typically, this involves asking questions.

PERSONAL REFLECTION

Why do teachers ask so many questions? Add as many reasons as you can to the following three, then think of what alternatives there are to asking questions.

- To encourage students to respond
- To provide feedback
- To check understanding

Language classrooms are dominated by question-and-answer routines. Very often, teachers know the answers to the questions they ask; these are known as **display questions**, since their function is primarily to get learners to display what they know or to check understanding. In everyday life outside the classroom, people rarely ask display questions (though caregivers may do this in interaction with little children learning their first language); they are a distinctive feature of classroom interaction. Examples of display questions are: 'what's the past tense of go?'; 'what's this girl wearing?' (Figure 6.2). Display questions often underpin the practice stage of the PPP methodology described in Chapter 4.

Responses to display questions are typically short, just one or two words. While they are a useful means of getting and giving feedback, display questions do not produce longer, more engaged responses. To generate longer answers, promote discussion and debate, and involve learners more evenly in the interaction, teachers turn to genuine questions, called **referential questions**. Referential questions

Figure 6.2 Asking the right question.
Source: Image © Áine Walsh 2023.

often begin with a *wh-* question such as *who, why, what, when, where,* or *which.* They often result in a more conversational kind of interaction, where students play a more equal role and have more opportunities to participate freely.

Extracts 6.2 and 6.3 illustrate the use of display and referential questions, respectively. In Extract 6.2, a class of low intermediate–level students are answering questions designed to help them recap a story.

EXTRACT 6.2

T: no if you look at the first sentence Liyan can you read the first sentence please
L3: lot of gold in the sea
T: uhuh and then the LAST sentence [reading] 'the treasure in the ocean might just as well not exist'. what treasure? . . . Ying?
L2: in the seawater
T: yes yeah so the SEAwater is another name for? . . . in this case? another way of saying . . . what? Cheng?
L1: ocean
T: ocean right and what's in the ocean . . . treasure and what's in the seawater?
LL: gold

(Walsh 2006)

In Extract 6.2, participation and learner responses are tightly controlled by the teacher, whose goal is simply to recap and check understanding through the use of display questions. In lines 1, 5, 8, and 10, the teacher gets students to display what they already know from what they have read. Learner responses are short, typically two or three words, and there is no space for topic development. From this short extract, we can conclude that the teacher's pedagogic goal was to check comprehension; her use of display questions is appropriate.

In Extract 6.3, on the other hand, we notice very different interaction patterns. In this extract, the teacher is working with a more advanced group, preparing to read a text on the supernatural. The interaction looks more like a casual conversation, with learners participating actively and giving fuller, more complex responses.

EXTRACT 6.3

T: I agree do you do you believe in this kind of stuff? We talked
     about UFOs and stuff yesterday (2)
L3: no . . . well maybe . . .
T: maybe no why not? (7)
L3: um I'm not a religious person and that's the thing I associate
     with religion and believe in supernaturals and things like that
     and believe in god's will and that's so far from me so no
T: I understand so and why maybe Monica?
L4: well, I'm also not connected with religion but maybe also
     something exists but I erm am rather sceptical but maybe peo-
     ple who have experienced things maybe=
T: uh huh and what about you . . . do you
L4: so

                                                        (Walsh 2006)

The teacher's opening question is a referential one. His goal is to get
the students' opinions, and initially he receives a short response in
line 3. The teacher then seeks clarification (*why not*), waits for seven
seconds (indicated (7) at line 4), and is rewarded with a much longer
response in lines 5–7. Note how the combined use of 'why' and 7
seconds of wait time produce a longer, more complex response. A
similar pattern follows with a question and longer response from
Monica in lines 9–11. The teacher's strategy of asking referential
questions, seeking clarification, and allowing thinking time results in
a more conversational, loosely controlled exchange. Given that his
intended (stated) goal at this stage of the lesson was to improve *fluency*, the strategy is appropriate. Notably, the conversation includes
elements of both fluency and complexity in the fluency-accuracy-complexity triangle discussed in previous chapters.

   The interactions in Extracts 6.2 and 6.3 are noticeably different:
short, tightly controlled learner responses are seen in 6.2, with longer, fuller, more complex responses in 6.3. The answers teachers
get depend very much on the questions asked; genuine (referential)
questions prompt more involved and active student participation.

   Apart from asking questions, teachers spend a great deal of time
correcting errors, the third of our four features. Error correction,
also known as *repair* (or sometimes generally referred to as *corrective*

feedback; see Chapter 5), may take several forms, and teachers are always faced with a decision when correcting students' mistakes. The basic choices are:

- Ignore the error.
- Indicate that an error has been made and correct it.
- Indicate that an error has been made and get that student to correct it.
- Indicate that an error has been made and get other students to correct it (peer correction).

There are many debates about when, why, and how errors should be corrected; some activities need more error correction, others less. A controlled grammar or vocabulary activity where accuracy is the focus will probably need more error correction than an open class discussion or pronunciation issues that do not affect fluency or intelligibility.

RESEARCH EVIDENCE

Students do expect to have their errors corrected. Work by Paul Seed-house (1997) confirms this: 'making linguistic errors and having them corrected directly and overtly is not an embarrassing matter' (571). In Chapter 5, we also referred to Penny Ur's survey of students' attitudes to error correction (2012: 91–94).

The final feature of classroom interaction is *speech modification*. Teachers modify their speech by using simpler structures, slowing their speed of delivery, speaking more loudly and clearly, and using a more restricted range of vocabulary, in other words, a feature of *audience design* (see the discussions in Chapter 2). Teachers also make greater use of multimodal features such as gestures, gaze, eye contact, head nods, and so on.

Teachers need to be understood; learners will make very little progress if they can't understand the teacher: understanding always comes before learning. Teachers spend a lot of time modelling language: using appropriate pronunciation, stress, and intonation. Acting as a model for language is an important part of being an English language teacher (Figure 6.3).

One of the biggest difficulties for students is 'keeping up'. Classrooms are busy places, where the flow of a lesson is often fast paced and challenging for anyone using English as an L2. Using an 'instructional voice' helps students to follow the lesson and feel they are being included. An important part of helping students to 'navigate the discourse' (Breen 1998) is the use of discourse markers. Words like *right, ok, now, so, alright, well* signal changes in the focus of a lesson or transitions from one stage to the next. They help learners 'find their way' in the interaction, functioning like punctuation marks in a written text. Research on turn-opening items in classroom interaction (e.g., Evison 2013), for example, has shown that *okay* performs a whole range of functions: marking transitions, holding student attention, checking comprehension, giving feedback, and so on. In a work examining discourse markers used by supervisors in one-to-one sessions with students, Samir Bakeer shows how bodily gestures align with the use of discourse markers to support illocutionary intent (Bakeer 2023: ch.8). Essentially,

Figure 6.3 Teachers are language models.
Source: Image © Áine Walsh 2023.

teachers use language more consciously; more deliberately; and with a greater use of pausing, emphasis, and body language.

Other more subtle strategies that teachers use to clarify, check, or confirm meanings are also evident. These include confirmation checks, where teachers make sure they understand learners; comprehension checks, ensuring that learners understand the teacher; repetition; clarification requests, asking students for clarification; reformulation, rephrasing a learner's utterance; turn completion, finishing a learner's contribution; and backtracking, returning to an earlier part of a dialogue. These strategies are used to ensure that the discourse flows and that the complex relationship between language use and learning is maintained.

A teacher's ability to modify their speech is one of the hallmarks of good teaching. Effective speech modification ensures that learners feel safe and included and gives them the confidence to participate in the interaction. It also minimises breakdowns and misunderstandings, stresses community identity (Chapter 5), and creates a sense of purposeful dialogue in which a group of learners is engaged in collective activity.

EASY AS 1, 2, 3

Classroom interaction follows a typical structure. The three-part exchange structure IRF is sometimes known as **IRE**. IRE is used to highlight that the feedback teachers give is often an evaluation (E) of a student's contribution. IRF is also known as a **recitation script** or **triadic structure** (*triadic* refers to the three moves: a question, a response, and a follow-up).

Extract 6.4 illustrates the structure.

EXTRACT 6.4

T: So, can you read question two, Junya.	**I**
L1: (*Reading from book*) Where was Sabina when this happened?	**R**
T: Right, yes, where was Sabina. In Unit 10, where was she?	**F/I**
L1: Er, go out . . .	**R**
T: She went out, yes.	**F**

(Walsh 2014)

Extract 6.4 opens with the discourse marker *so*; as already mentioned, discourse markers are used frequently to mark transitions to new phases of a lesson. The opening remark, or pre-initiation (line 1), leads to the question in line 1, prompting the response (R) in line 2. In line 3, the teacher offers feedback (F): *right yes*. In l.3, the teacher seeks further clarification and receives the response *she go out*, which is then acknowledged and corrected in the feedback move (line 5).

The IRF exchange structure fulfils several functions:

- It illustrates the special nature of classroom interaction.
- It shows why teacher talk is so frequent: for every utterance made by a learner, teachers typically make two.
- It illustrates how, if overused, classroom interaction could become mechanical and monotonous.
- It helps in identifying other types of interaction (see the discussion on self evaluation of teacher talk (SETT) subsequently).

SETT: SELF EVALUATION OF TEACHER TALK

The IRF exchange structure is the basic building block of classroom interaction. When we examine longer stretches of interaction, however, different patterns emerge, allowing us to identify specific interactional features such as clarification request, content feedback, and so on. The SETT framework attempts to achieve a closer understanding of teacher talk at a level of discourse beyond the three-part exchange.

The SETT framework comprises four classroom micro-contexts (called **modes**) and 13 interactional features (called **interactures**). Each mode has a different pedagogic focus and uses different interactional features. Modes recognise that a teacher's language use varies according to their goal; for example, setting up an activity uses instructional language, checking, and discourse markers to signpost the interaction. Promoting a class discussion, on the other hand, requires greater use of referential questions, clarification requests, and extended learner turns. SETT recognises that all language lessons are made up of a series of micro-contexts (modes) which are co-constructed by teachers and learners through their interactions.

Each mode has clearly defined pedagogic goals and interactional features (interactures) (see also Seedhouse 2004). A mode is defined as 'an L2 classroom micro-context which has a clearly defined pedagogic goal and distinctive interactional features determined largely by a teacher's use of language' (Walsh 2006: 134). The definition is intended to emphasise the idea that interaction and classroom activity are inextricably linked, and to acknowledge that as the focus of a lesson changes, interaction patterns and pedagogic goals change too.

The four modes, together with their interactional features and typical pedagogic goals, are summarised in Table 6.1.

Table 6.1 L2 classroom modes (Walsh 2013).

Mode	Pedagogic Goals	Interactional Features
Managerial	• transmit information • organise the physical learning environment • refer learners to materials • introduce or conclude an activity • change from one mode of learning to another	• a single, extended teacher turn using explanations and/or instructions • transitional markers • confirmation checks • absence of learner contributions
Materials	• provide language practice around a piece of material • elicit responses in relation to the material • check and display answers • clarify when necessary • evaluate contributions	• predominance of IRF • display questions • form-focused feedback • corrective repair • scaffolding
Skills and systems	• enable learners to produce correct forms • enable learners to manipulate the target language • provide corrective feedback • provide learners with practice in sub-skills • display correct answers	• direct repair • scaffolding • extended teacher turns • display questions • teacher echo • clarification requests • form-focused feedback
Classroom context	• helps learners to express themselves clearly • establish a context • promote oral fluency	• extended learner turns • short teacher turns • minimal repair • content feedback • referential questions • scaffolding • clarification requests

The following sub-sections, which give an overview of the SETT modes, include extracts taken from Walsh (2006).

Managerial mode covers how learning and learning activities are organised in time and space. It typically occurs at the beginning and end of a lesson, task, or activity. It comprises a single, extended teacher turn, with little or no learner involvement. There are frequent repetitions, instructions, and checking of understanding. At the end of managerial mode, there is typically a handing over to learners and a movement to another mode; in Extract 6.5, for example, the words 'so Miguel' act as a transition to another mode (skills and systems). Discourse markers such as *ok, so, now,* and *right* help learners to follow what is said and give direction to the discourse.

EXTRACT 6.5

T: Ok we're going to look today at ways to improve your writing and at ways which can be more effective for you and if you look at the writing which I gave you back you will see that I've marked any little mistakes and eh I've also marked places where I think the writing is good and I haven't corrected your mistakes because the best way in writing is for you to correct your mistakes so what I have done I have put little circles and inside the circles there is something which tells you what kind of mistake it is so Miguel would you like to tell me one of the mistakes that you made.

When managerial mode occurs at the beginning of a lesson, the teacher's main concern is to 'locate' the learning both in time and space using phrases like 'ok, now you remember last time . . .?', 'if you could look now at page 64 . . . ', and so on. Once learning has been located, learners are invited to participate: *so Miguel, would you like to tell me one of the mistakes that you made.* Locating learning is a first step in creating a context, and managerial mode functions as a support to the other three modes. It is an 'enabling' mode (McCarthy and Walsh 2003).

MATERIALS MODE

In this mode, all interaction typically centres around a piece of material such as a text, audio or video resource, or worksheet. In most cases, the interaction is tightly controlled and follows the IRF exchange structure. In Extract 6.6, the interaction is almost entirely determined by the materials and managed by the teacher. Teacher and learner turns follow a classic IRF sequence: each teacher turn provides an evaluation of a learner's contribution and initiation of another one. The teacher's goal is to practice vocabulary; key items are elicited, confirmed, and displayed by the teacher through echoes of a previous contribution. Display questions dominate, and learners respond with short, single-word, or brief responses.

EXTRACT 6.6

T: now . . . see if you can find the words that are suitable in in these phrases [starts reading] in the world cup final of 1994 Brazil Italy 2, 3 2 and in a shoot-out . . . what words would you put in there?
L7: beat
T: what . . . beat Italy 3 2 yeah in?
L7: in a penalty shoot-out
T: a what?
L7: in a penalty shoot-out
T: in a penalty shoot-out very good in a penalty shoot-out . . .

SKILLS AND SYSTEMS MODE

In many ways, skills and systems mode is like materials mode; typically, the interaction follows IRF. The difference is that the pedagogic focus is on a particular language system (vocabulary, grammar, phonology, discourse) or skill (reading, writing, listening, speaking). The focus is on accuracy rather than fluency, and teachers may correct errors more actively than in other modes. Scaffolding, where new vocabulary or grammar are fed into the interaction, is also widely found in this mode.

We see an example of skills and systems mode in Extract 6.7, where a group of intermediate students is practicing irregular simple past forms (*went* and *broke*).

EXTRACT 6.7

L5: the good news is he went to the went to . . .
T: he went to what do we call these things the shoes with wheels
L2: ah skates
L6: roller skates
T: ROLLer skates roller skates so he went
L5: he went to
L: roller SKATing
T: SKATing
L5: he went to
T: not to just he went roller skating he went roller skating
L5: roller skating he went roller skating

The extract opens with L5 responding to a previous teacher question. In line 2, the teacher scaffolds L5 (*what do we call these things the shoes with wheels*) and elicits two correct responses in lines 3 and 4. These responses are confirmed by the teacher in line 5, who then initiates another response (*so he went*). Note also how the teacher stresses syllables (in capitals) to direct attention to correct forms. L5's contribution in line 9 is then corrected by the teacher using **direct repair** in line 10. This combination of scaffolding and direct repair is found extensively in skills and systems mode. It allows learners to deal with specific problems or mistakes in their contribution while allowing teachers to keep the lesson on track.

CLASSROOM CONTEXT MODE

In classroom context mode, the interaction looks more like casual conversation. Opportunities for genuine communication are frequent, and the teacher plays a less prominent role, taking more of a back seat. In this mode, referential questions are used more actively, while direct repair is less common. The teacher's role is to manage the discourse and allow students all the interactional space they need.

In Extract 6.8, a group of advanced learners has been invited to share their experiences of the supernatural.

EXTRACT 6.8

L3: ahh nah the one thing that happens when a person dies (unintelligible) my mother used to work with old people and when they died . . . the last thing that went out was the hearing about this person

T: aha (2)

L3: so I mean even if you are unconscious or on drugs or something I mean it's probably still perhaps can hear what's happened (2)

L2: but it gets

LL: but it gets/there are

L3: I mean you have seen so many operation ((3)) and so you can imagine and when you are hearing the sounds of what happens I think you can get a pretty clear picture of what's really going on there

In Extract 6.8, the teacher contributes only once (line 4). Learners manage the interaction themselves, produce longer turns, and engage in what looks much like a conversation. Errors go unchecked, there are no evaluative comments, and the only feedback given is content based, normally in the shape of a personal reaction. The students are free to say what they want, when they want. Giving students more control of topic is known as '**topicalisation**' (Slimani 1992). When learners have control of topic, they are more likely to learn something: 'whatever is topicalised by the learners rather than the teacher has a better chance of being claimed to have been learnt' (Ellis 1998: 159).

We turn now to a closer description of the interactional features of SETT, called *interactures*. Table 6.2 shows how the four modes are made up of 13 interactures and a number of clearly defined pedagogic goals (see Walsh 2002, 2006, 2011, 2013 for further details).

The interactures used in the SETT framework can be found in any classroom; they are intended to be representative rather than exhaustive and do not claim to describe all teacher talk. Some are more common than others and occur with greater regularity; display questions, for example, are more widespread than referential, or genuine, questions. Display questions are also more frequent in lower-level classes.

Table 6.2 SETT interactures.

Interacture	Description
Scaffolding	1. Reformulation (rephrasing a learner's contribution).
	2. Extension (extending a learner's contribution).
	3. Modelling (providing an example for learner(s).
Direct repair	Correcting an error quickly and directly.
Content feedback	Giving feedback to the message rather than the words used.
Extended wait time	Allowing sufficient time for students to respond or formulate a response.
Referential question	Genuine questions to which the teacher doesn't know the answer.
Seeking clarification	1. Teacher asks a student to clarify something the student has said.
	2. Student asks teacher to clarify something the teacher has said.
Extended learner turn	A longer learner turn of more than one utterance.
Teacher echo	1. Teacher repeats their previous utterance.
	2. Teacher repeats a learner's contribution.
Teacher interruptions	Interrupting a learner' contribution.
Extended teacher turn	Teacher turn of more than one utterance.
Turn completion	Completing a learner's contribution for the learner.
Display question	Asking questions to which teacher knows the answer.
Form-focused feedback	Giving feedback on the words used, not the message.

The interactures are triggered in particular modes at appropriate moments in the lesson (Figure 6.4). Certain interactures are more *appropriate* to a particular mode: clarification requests, for example, are typically found in classroom context mode, whereas teacher interruptions may be found in skills and systems mode. An interacture, then, can be defined as a particular interactional feature which belongs to or is typical of a specific mode. An interacture can be regarded as being more or less appropriate at a given moment in a lesson according to the desired learning outcomes.

Figure 6.4 Modes and interactures.
Source: Image © Áine Walsh 2023.

Here is what one teacher said about their use of the framework:

> It will be interesting to see whether the features that I identified most clearly were a mixture of reformulation and direct repair, extended wait time, echo, form-focused feedback, turn completion. Now I think I think in the context that was fairly appropriate, but I think I would be inclined to do that when it's NOT necessary and I'd be interested to see if that's a feature of a different kind of lesson.

(Walsh 2006)

PERSONAL REFLECTION

Think about how you might use SETT in teaching. Questions to consider:

1. Would you make a video recording or ask a colleague to observe you?
2. Which modes would you focus on?
3. Are there any interactures which you'd like to use more actively or use less?
4. How might you change your teaching after using SETT?

COULD DO BETTER (CIC)

We have seen that interaction is 'where the action is': it is crucial to teaching and learning, it provides teachers and learners with feedback on their development, and it lies at the heart of everything we do in a language classroom. In short, the goal is classroom interactional competence (CIC), defined as 'teachers' and learners' ability to use interaction as a tool for mediating and assisting learning' (Walsh 2013: 130).

As we have seen in the previous section, reflective frameworks like SETT can foster a teacher's awareness of their use of language. All teachers have engrained habits which are carried into the classroom, such as the tendency to repeat everything (teacher echo) or a failure to wait long enough after asking a question (wait time). We can refer to these speech habits as our *classroom idiolect*: our own personal and individual way of communicating while teaching. It is good to be aware of these behaviours and observe the ways in which they impact learner involvement and engagement. For example, the discourse marker *okay* can potentially be over-used by the teacher; this said, it performs a range of functions such as checking understanding, getting attention, concluding a task or activity, and so on. Understanding how discourse markers function is one aspect of CIC.

CORPUS EVIDENCE

Using a corpus, we can identify which two-, three-, and four-word combinations of words occur in classrooms and how they function. The following are the 12 most frequent three-word combinations in the LIBEL corpus of university seminar interactions (Limerick and Belfast corpus).

1. A lot of	7. A couple of
2. And so on	8. A little bit
3. I don't know	9. A bit of
4. At the moment	10. As I said
5. In other words	11. First of all
6. A number of	12. As well as
	(Adapted from Walsh and O'Keeffe 2007)

Many of these chunks signpost the interaction and help learners find their way through the discourse. Helping learners in this way is an aspect of CIC.

When we analyse classroom transcripts, it is clear that levels of CIC vary from one context to another and from one teacher to another. Some teachers manage the interaction so that learning and learning opportunities are maximised. Others display interactional behaviour that can impede opportunities for learning and restrict learner participation (Walsh 2002). For example, the overuse of display questions can result in a string of simple, short responses from learners and restrict engagement and participation.

Teachers demonstrate CIC in a number of ways, for example, ensuring that language use and pedagogic goals are working together. The SETT framework allows us to evaluate the appropriateness of our talk at any given moment in a lesson. Other features of CIC include extended wait time (allowing a reasonable amount of time after asking a question and not interrupting students) and extending learner responses (e.g., paraphrasing a learner's utterance), scaffolding a contribution, offering a key piece of vocabulary, or introducing a new phrase as and when needed.

Questions to consider in relation to developing a closer understanding of classroom interaction include:

- How does task-type affect interaction? Do some tasks promote more interaction, others less?
- How does a task create or restrict opportunities for learning?
- How might more effective management of interaction lead to dialogic teaching (Mercer 2008)?
- What can we do to maximise interaction?
- How does a teacher's feedback affect learner participation?

CONCLUSION

This chapter has discussed the importance of interaction in teaching and learning, arguing that becoming an effective teacher depends very much on an ability to make good use of language and communication while teaching. One of the hallmarks of good teaching is making good moment-by-moment decisions. One way of making the right decisions at the right moment is to develop closer understandings of the relationship between language, interaction, and learning.

The SETT framework was introduced as a tool for reflecting on, evaluating, and improving classroom interaction. SETT is made up of four classroom modes and 14 interactures, or interactional features. The tool can be used to reflect on, describe, and evaluate teaching in relation to CIC. In Chapter 7, we consider how teachers might become more competent by reflecting on and developing their professional practice.

FURTHER READING

Jenks, C. 2021. *Researching Classroom Discourse: A Student Guide.* **Abingdon, Oxon and New York: Routledge**.
This guide to researching classroom discourse will be of interest to researchers and teachers alike. It offers a step-by-step guide to studying classroom interaction and is written in a clear style which makes even the most complex features accessible.

Sert, O. 2015. *Social Interaction and L2 Classroom Discourse.* **Edinburgh: Edinburgh University Press**.
This comprehensive book provides a detailed investigation of classroom discourse using a conversation analytic methodology. The book covers the various interactional practices teachers use in second language classrooms, including both verbal and non-verbal actions.

Walsh, S. 2011. Second edition due 2025. *Exploring Classroom Discourse: Language in Action.* **Abingdon, Oxon: Routledge**.
This book offers a fuller description of the main ideas presented in this chapter. It introduces and exemplifies the SETT framework and offers a comprehensive discussion of CIC.

Walsh, S. 2014. *Classroom Interaction for Language Teachers.* **Virginia, USA: TESOL Press**.
The book covers different approaches to interaction in the language classroom, providing a guide to understanding interaction and its challenges for teachers. The book is aimed at beginning and early career teachers and offers a short introduction to the field.

7

LEARNING HOW TO DO IT
TEACHER EDUCATION

ELTE PATHWAYS

In this chapter, we turn our attention to English language teacher education (**ELTE**). As in any profession, there are accreditation bodies, training providers, educational institutions, evaluation agencies, and so on who ensure that standards are established and maintained. For English language teachers, qualifications are offered at initial and in-service levels, aimed at novice, early career, and experienced teachers. Given that learning to teach is a lifelong enterprise, there are also less formal, more individualised contexts for **continuing professional development** (**CPD**), where teachers develop through experiential learning, action research, and reflective practice.

WHAT TEACHERS SAY

A good way of finding out what it's like to teach is to talk to teachers. We invited two teachers to comment on their experiences by asking them these questions:

1. What do you most/least like about your job as an EFL teacher?
2. Recall your first teaching job: how well prepared did you feel? What challenges did you face, and how did you overcome them?

Martin is a university lecturer with many years' ELT experience. He said:

1. Most liked: Teaching higher levels and exploring the language with the students; working in an environment where

DOI: 10.4324/9781003350316-7

teachers shared ideas and actually got excited about lesson plans. . . . Least liked: 'conversation' classes, especially one-to-one or small groups; teaching children; teaching some grammar areas; endlessly searching for activities to keep students (customers) entertained.

2. Totally unprepared, had no training. Followed the instructions in the teacher's book line-by-line. Read the units just ahead of the students to learn the grammar. Fell back on some general teaching tips I picked up on my BEd (e.g., some drama activities). Totally unsuitable for EFL teaching. Or at least had no idea why I was using them.

Some of Martin's comments are widespread; most teachers have preferences about teaching language forms versus teaching skills. Martin enjoys working with the language and is less comfortable teaching skills. Similarly, teachers often have preferences about teaching different levels and age groups. Martin enjoys teaching advanced adult learners and has a less positive attitude towards EYL. Note his concerns about activities to 'keep customers entertained'. This is a common reaction from experienced teachers; there is a sense in some quarters that the role of the teacher is to entertain students through a range of tasks and activities.

Another teacher, Ruth, looked back on her first ELT job. She told us she had 'a great range of experience of students of different backgrounds and levels'. On the negative side, she too felt ill prepared – she came to the job with a UK school teaching qualification to teach French and found ELT to be quite different, but 'I probably had enough confidence at the time to approach it'.

PERSONAL REFLECTION

What are/were the priorities for you as a teacher in terms of preparation for the job? Which aspects of teaching do you feel you need(ed) most support with?

GETTING STARTED: PRESET

CELTA

By far the most popular, most widely accepted, and most comprehensive pre-service teacher education (**PRESET**) qualification is
the Certificate in English Language Teaching to Adults (**CELTA**) –
now officially called Certificate in Teaching English to Speakers of
Other Languages. The CELTA, offered across 300 centres and 54
countries, is typically taken as an intensive four-week course. For
many English language teachers, it is the only qualification they
ever obtain. There are two main providers validating this kind of
qualification: Cambridge Assessment validates the CELTA, while
Trinity College London validates the Certificate in TESOL.

INFORMATION ADD-ON

Full details of CELTA can be found at: www.cambridgeenglish.org/teach-
ing-english/teaching-qualifications/celta/, and details of the Trinity Certificate at: www.trinitycollege.com/qualifications/teaching-english/
CertTESOL.

It is possible nowadays to take both these courses online, though there's
considerable merit in opting for the face-to-face versions. Both courses
offer around 120 hours of training and include 6 hours of supervised
teaching practice. Student teachers (STs) take part in group discussions
after each teaching practice session. These discussions, called post-ob-
servation conferences (**POCs**), are both highly formative and challenging; STs' performance is evaluated individually by peers and by the
trainer leading the session (Figure 7.1). There are obvious tensions in
this context, where the aim is to offer an appropriate amount of support while assessing a ST's teaching. As Roberts (1998: 161) tells us:
'[the issue is] to build the most open and supportive relationship possible while also applying course criteria and challenging students'.

While it is generally accepted that reflection on initial teacher
training courses is crucial (Farr 2006), there have been studies which
highlight a mismatch between the stated aims of the course and the

Figure 7.1 POC. All about feedback.
Source: Image © Áine Walsh 2023.

Table 7.1 CELTA teaching practice feedback (adapted from Mann and Walsh 2017).

Comments on plan	Your plan is fine and shows logical staging.
Strengths	You seem much more confident this week and you set up the listening well.
Areas for development	Overall, this was a nice skills lesson. It's a shame that you didn't use the opportunity to teach some vocabulary related to the topic.
	Make sure that you have sufficient material in your plan for purposeful learning and keep an ear open so that learners are on-task even when you are not near them. This was a much stronger lesson than last week – well done. Aim to teach some grammar in your next lesson.

interactions which take place in practice (e.g., Copland 2012). In some cases, for example, trainees simply want to be told what they should be doing rather than trying to work it out themselves.

The kind of feedback which is typically given after a teaching practice session is shown in Table 7.1.

The feedback in Table 7.1 is a mix of positive and critical comment, suggestions for improvement, and aims for the next teaching session. Note, too, that feedback is often written; student teachers are also asked to complete their own reflective commentary, also in writing.

The POC is probably the most challenging and, at the same time, most developmental component of the CELTA course. It gives trainees an opportunity to give and receive feedback on each other's teaching and benefit from the comments and advice of an experienced teacher educator. The skill of the trainer is in allowing STs to have space for reflection and in promoting an open and focused dialogue which is both honest and accurate. As Waring (2013) points out, STs are not 'recipients' of the feedback; they play a role in co-constructing mutual understanding. After six hours of supervised teaching practice, most trainee teachers gain the skills and confidence they will need to embark on a career as an English language teacher.

BY DEGREES: BA AND MA

Other qualifications include MA in TESOL degrees, which are offered in a number of countries and aimed at initial teacher education. In addition, there exists a smaller number of BA TESOL/ELT degrees across universities worldwide. All these courses are much longer than the standard four-week CELTA; BA degrees are typically three years, while most MA TESOL degrees last 12 months. The advantage of a longer course is that there is more time to acquire a deeper understanding of teaching and learning and to develop key skills. Where courses include a teaching practice component, there may also be an attachment to a school, which can offer opportunities for professional development and learning from experienced teachers. There are also some disadvantages of taking a degree course, the main ones being the time taken to gain a qualification, the cost, and the fact that they may be less practical than certificate-level courses.

Other English-speaking countries like Australia and the United States offer their own brands of initial ELTE courses which are comparable to CELTA. For example, in Australia, it's possible to take the Certificate IV in TESOL, accredited by the Australian government, as a qualification for individuals wishing to teach ESL to students in Australia and overseas. In the United States, many universities offer their own certificate courses for students who would like to teach either in the United States or overseas. Further details can be found here: www.academiccourses.com/certificate/tesol/usa.

Initial, pre-service (PRESET) teacher education is both the most challenging and most important context for becoming an English language teacher. There will be face-threatening moments for anyone learning to teach, since what is being assessed is an individual's performance. There's no single right way to teach; good teachers come in all guises, with different personalities, approaches to teaching, and beliefs about how languages are learned. A key challenge for trainee and early career teachers is to learn how to develop and grow through experience and in dialogue with colleagues. Newly qualified teachers can hone their skills by using evidence from the classroom, by talking to peers and sharing ideas, and by developing a close understanding of the context in which they work.

KEEPING GOING: INSET

DELTA

If the CELTA is often the preferred qualification for initial teacher education, the Diploma in English Language Teaching to Adults (**DELTA**) is one of the most popular qualifications for in-service teacher education (**INSET**). It is also offered by Cambridge Assessment, which claims:

> [The DELTA] is one of the best-known and most popular advanced TEFL/TESOL qualifications in the world. It can be taken at any stage in a teacher's career and is ideal for those wanting to update their teaching knowledge and improve their practice.
> (www.cambridgeenglish.org/teaching-english/teaching-qualifications/delta)

One of the most innovative DELTAs in the United Kingdom is offered at Leeds Beckett University as part of an MA in TESOL. It was set up by Heather Buchanan and Ivor Timmis. In an interview,

Ivor and Heather were asked to comment on their understanding of reflection. Ivor said:

> We try to get them to look at actual evidence, things like getting them to record a little bit of that class and then go back and do something analytical with it, something like go back and listen to the instructions that you gave, we try to make it as evidence based as we can.
>
> (Mann and Walsh 2017: 86).

Ivor's position (and the thinking behind the DELTA) is that teachers need to make use of data and evidence in their practice. Rather than relying on subjective comments about what went well and what didn't go well in a teaching session, evidence from actual practice is used as a springboard for reflection.

In most INSET programmes, teachers are encouraged to think about their current approach to teaching and consider how they might like to develop. A key element of DELTA course work is the reflective portfolio, which requires teachers to write commentaries about their practice, describing one aspect of their teaching, such as presenting vocabulary, and considering how they might like to change things in the future. This process of reflective writing allows time for thought, for discussion with others and for considering practical options for change.

Gerald, a trainee on a DELTA programme offered and taught by Tony Wright, who used to work at the University of St Mark and St John, Plymouth, UK, wrote the following:

> The process of writing assignments and portfolios has given me an opportunity to verbalise my thoughts and refine my thinking. Writing also forces me to ask questions about my practice. The time between my drafts allowed me time to think through an idea or a problem because by writing a draft I had begun to put my ideas into tangible words. I felt that because I used writing as a thinking tool, it was easier to stay focused on the task. As far as professional development is concerned this is certainly true for me – nothing really existed until I began to write about it.
>
> (Adapted from Mann and Walsh 2017)

Writing about teaching entails reflection: the writing *is* the reflection, not simply evidence of it. And this practice can be extended to a range of contexts involving teachers and their students. For example, **learning logs** (where learners record their own experiences of learning L2) are a powerful means of gaining understanding of the complexities of teaching and learning and may result in 'light-bulb moments' (Figure 7.2), which are new understandings of old puzzles or issues.

PROFESSIONAL DEVELOPMENT 'IN THE WILD'

Teachers are not always able to take part in an INSET course like the DELTA. Much professional development takes place 'in the wild', on the job, informally, through gaining experience. Continuing professional development is the term used to denote any aspect of a teacher's professional development over their entire career. Much of this development may seem haphazard, unstructured, unsystematic, and almost accidental. There are no assignments, essays, reflective logs, or course requirements typical of those found in INSET programmes. Teachers

Figure 7.2 Light-bulb moments.
Source: Image © Áine Walsh 2023.

develop through **experiential learning** – by gaining experience, comparing ideas with colleagues, reading about professional practice, and so on. Of particular value is collaborative CPD, where teachers work together, either online or in person, to address a specific issue. Teachers develop new ideas, compare options, and discuss new practices through their interactions with other professionals.

RESEARCH EVIDENCE

According to Kennedy (2011), the benefits of collaborative CPD are:

- The process is informal, relying on interpersonal and communication skills.
- It is context-specific: teachers share and understand key issues.
- It takes place over a longer period, allowing space for dialogue and reflection.
- Confidence grows through interaction and discussion with peers.

A key element of any CPD process is evaluation. A range of tools and practices exists to help teachers understand and improve their practice. The British Council has established a framework to offer a structured and individualised approach to CPD. 'It is for teachers of all subjects [and] enables you to understand and plan your own professional development' (2015: 2). It is organised around four stages of development, moving from an elementary level of competence and knowledge to a more advanced stage:

1. Awareness: you have heard of this practice.
2. Understanding: you know what the practice means and why it's important
3. Engagement: you demonstrate competency in this practice.
4. Integration: you demonstrate a high level of competency in this practice which informs what you do at work.

There are a total of nine practices in the framework. The idea is that users may have different levels of competence in the various practices; for example, a high level of competency in lesson planning may be offset by a lower level in assessing learning. Full details of the framework can be found at: www.teachingenglish.org.uk/sites/teacheng/files/CPD%20framework%20for%20teachers_WEB.PDF.

The CPD framework allows teachers to develop at their own pace over time, focusing on specific areas of their professional practice. It promotes reflection, collaboration with colleagues, and discussion about teaching and learning. The framework also underlines that teacher education is a lifelong process for which the individual teacher assumes full responsibility.

The British Council offers a wealth of materials, resources, suggestions about 'how to', and other information on their *Teaching English* webpages.[1]

THINKING IT THROUGH

PERSONAL REFLECTION

Thinking back to your experiences as a language learner, which aspects of your experience would benefit from reflection? How might teacher reflection have improved your experience as a learner? And how might your reflections have helped you as a language learner?

Reflective practice (RP) has been around since its inception by the American philosopher John Dewey in 1933. Dewey is often regarded as the father of reflection; he highlighted the importance of experiential learning and reflection as the 'sole method to escape from the purely impulsive or purely routine action' (1933: 15). He argued that teachers should not be passive recipients of knowledge but play an active role in designing materials, curricula, and teaching procedures. Dewey's work chimes with the main message of this book: learning – whether learning a language or learning to teach – requires a close understanding of the relationship between experience, interaction, and reflection. Reflection involves serious and determined engagement with a doubt or puzzle; it also involves testing hypotheses, or trying things out to see what works. Teaching can become very routine, almost mechanical. One of the challenges is to keep teaching fresh, to try out new ideas, introduce new activities, learn from experience, and so on.

For our purposes, we adopt the definition of reflection put forward by Boud et al. (1985: 3):

> [Reflection is] a generic term for those intellectual and affective activities in which individuals engage to explore their experiences in order to lead to new understandings and appreciation.

The key words in this definition are 'intellectual and affective activities', suggesting that reflection involves thought, instinct, intuition, and action, together with 'new understandings and appreciation'. Engaging in RP involves addressing a problem with a view to solving it or at least developing a closer understanding.

RP is often seen as a cycle (see, for example, Schön 1991; Kemmis and McTaggart 1988). The assumption is that the initial reflection stems from the classroom, from a teaching segment; this is then evaluated, and alternative teaching strategies or practices are explored and tried out.

Given its long history, there have been several criticisms of reflective practice, many of which have been discussed in recent publications (see, for example, Mann and Walsh 2013, 2017; Walsh and Mann 2015). The main criticisms, together with ways of dealing with them, are presented in Table 7.2.

Table 7.2 RP: problems and solutions.

Issue	Possible solution
Reflection is not based on evidence; typically, it involves subjective personal opinion.	Collect data from the classroom to use as a springboard for reflection.
RP is almost always written; there are few examples of spoken reflection.	Introduce **dialogic reflection**, where teachers reflect through talk and collaboration.
Reflection is often an individual activity.	Teachers reflect on their practice and share ideas.
Uses a very narrow range of tools, such as checklists and diaries.	Offer a wider range of **reflective tools**, such as video clips and 'stimulated recall'.
Teachers often don't know what to reflect *on* or what to reflect *with*.	RP should form a part of initial and in-service teacher education programmes.

A WAY FORWARD?

WHERE'S THE EVIDENCE?

When we look at accounts of reflection – the kinds of thing that student teachers use on initial teacher training courses, for example, we find models, checklists, prompt questions, and diaries. Typically, they are self-reports based on a teacher's own evaluation of their teaching.

Given the complexity of teaching, it is important that reflections use evidence so that they are reliable. The best form of evidence are data collected from teaching; a teacher's own data are a particularly rich resource grounded in their own context and experience (Walsh and Mann 2015). Data encourage honesty and a frank confrontation with problems. Consider the story of the student teacher who, while planning her teaching for the week, wrote her self-evaluations *before* she taught as a way of saving time and satisfying her course tutors. Valerie Hobbs talks about 'faking it': making claims which are simply not true and not based on evidence (2007).

Data, for the purposes of professional development and RP, could be anything at all which helps to understand teaching better. Examples might include a conversation with a student, a test result in which a class does much better or worse than expected, a piece of material, a task or activity, a discussion with a colleague. By using data, we access 'insider accounts' of teaching; we are able to reflect with greater confidence on what really happened.

It is easy with current technology to make short, 'snapshot' video clips which can then be used for reflection and discussion. That said, all ethical procedures must be followed to ensure that participants are protected; video recording is a highly sensitive practice, and permission to film and identity protection must be ensured at all times.

Extract 7.1 (adapted from Walsh and Mann 2015) is a video-recorded extract from a pre-sessional English class at a UK university. The teacher is eliciting responses about school memories from a group of eight adult intermediate learners.

EXTRACT 7.1

T: what was the funniest thing that happened to you at school . . .
    Tang?
S: funniest thing?
T: the funniest
S: the funniest thing I think out of school was go to picnic
T: go on a picnic? So what happened what made it funny?
S: go to picnic we made playing or talking with the teacher more
    closely because in the school we have a line you know he the
    teacher and me the student
T: so you say there was a gap or a wall between the teacher and the
    students so when you . . . if you go out of the school you went
    together with more (gestures 'closer' with hands) so you had a
    closer relationship outside the school
S: yeah yeah

In Extract 7.1, the teacher (T) is getting the class to reflect on
their school experiences. The interaction follows the IRF format, with the teacher asking questions and the student (S)
answering. There are errors which are ignored, as the teacher
wants to let the student express himself. In lines 8–10, the
teacher reformulates what the student has said to both check
understanding and make it clear for the class.

In Extract 7.2, the same teacher discussed this recording with
a colleague. He comments on the importance of **shaping** or
clarifying a student turn so that it is comprehensible for the class
as a whole.

EXTRACT 7.2

Basically, he's explaining that on a picnic there wasn't this gap that there
is in a classroom – psychological gap – that's what I'm drawing out of him.
There's a lot of scaffolding being done by me in this monitoring, besides it
being managerial, there's a lot of scaffolding because I want to get it flowing, I want to encourage them, keep it moving as it were. I'm clarifying to
the class what he's saying because I know in an extended turn – a broken
turn – and it's not exactly fluent and it's not articulate – I try to

re-interpret for the benefit of the class so that they're all coming with me at the same time, and they all understand the point being made by him.

(Adapted from Walsh and Mann 2015)

The teacher's reflections are probably more detailed than they might have been without this data. They are also more accurate and reliable since they use evidence from the recording. The teacher makes a number of observations about his use of scaffolding, the lack of error correction to 'keep it flowing', and the need to 'interpret for the benefit of the class'.

IT'S GOOD TO TALK

RP is often viewed as an individual process, something done alone (Figure 7.3), possibly in a darkened room at the end of a week's teaching! This view of RP is common in current approaches to teacher education. Unfortunately, it perpetuates the idea that teaching is about solo performance and that professional development is best done alone.

Figure 7.3 Reflecting alone.
Source: Image © Áine Walsh 2023.

We learn through talk, as we discussed in Chapter 3 under the heading of socio-cultural theory (SCT). Yet SCT applies as much to teacher education as to language learning (see, for example, Johnson 2009). Learning to teach is a social process which is mediated by language and interaction (Johnson and Golombek 2011). Throughout the process, reflection is an active phenomenon involving dialogue rather than solitary, inward-looking thought (Figure 7.3).

The CELTA advocates the value of learning from others' experiences in its use of the post-lesson group feedback session. Collaborating and learning from others is very much in line with Dewey's original formulation of reflection, which highlighted cooperation and dialogue.

We mentioned that most forms of reflection involve writing (see, for example, Farrell 2013). While there is nothing inherently wrong with written reflection, there is perhaps a need to re-balance this practice and introduce spoken reflection. There are several reasons for this:

- For many student teachers, reflection is a course requirement to complete a teacher training course or to pass an assignment (McCabe et al. 2009). We have seen how this can lead to problems such as 'faking it' (Hobbs 2007).
- Most initial and in-service teacher education programmes, like CELTA and DELTA, use standard forms or checklists. Teachers often focus more on completing the checklist, ticking the boxes, than reflecting on practice.
- Repeated use of checklists and forms may result in a mechanical approach to reflection. If these forms are not graded, they have potentially little or no surrender value.
- There is the question of whether reflection should be assessed.

A possible way forward, and one which can be facilitated through technology, is dialogic reflection, involving teachers in a collaborative dialogue about a specific piece of teaching. By using snapshot video clips, teachers have an opportunity to discuss their teaching, describe what happened, think of possible explanations, and discuss alternatives. This approach offers deeper, richer articulation and analysis of a segment of teaching; it is also more likely to result in professional benefit. The teacher educator Julian Edge advocates **cooperative development**, involving a *Speaker* and an *Understander*. The Speaker comments on their practice, possibly a specific issue or puzzle; the goal of the Understander is to reflect back their understanding and to help the Speaker clarify their thinking. The process typically results in **deep** rather than **surface reflection** (Edge 2002, and see https://cooperative-development.com/?page_id=110).

An example of dialogic reflection is shown in Extract 7.4. Here, two teachers, Mike and Joy, are discussing a teaching segment involving scaffolding. They have analysed the recording using SETT and are now discussing their evaluation. This extract is taken from an audio recording of their discussion.

EXTRACT 7.3

Mike: Is scaffolding something you think you do more of in that type of mode for example you're in a skills and systems mode here. Do you think it's something that happens more in some modes than others or is it maybe too difficult to say at this stage?

Joy: My first feeling would be yes because it's so focused on language that anything they give me that might not be correct and not clear then I'm going to re-formulate it or anything they don't understand I'm going to give them a lot of examples so that's all scaffolding isn't it?

(Adapted from Walsh and Mann 2015)

Joy reflects on her use of scaffolding, possibly for the first time. Her comments suggest that she is trying to understand it herself, both in terms of what it means (*so that's all scaffolding isn't it?*) and how it is used (*I'm going to reformulate it*). Mike plays a key role in this extract: he helps Joy to clarify her own reflections, understand when a particular practice occurs, and explain why.

Dialogic reflection involves teachers reflecting *through* dialogue to arrive at a closer understanding of their teaching and, importantly, to be in a position to articulate their understanding. In any process of reflection, there are a number of key stages which are assisted by dialogue:

1. Describe what happened.
2. Say why.
3. Analyse and evaluate.
4. Consider alternatives.
5. Discuss future actions.

THE RIGHT TOOLS FOR THE JOB

Current approaches to RP tend to rely on a rather narrow range of tools such as checklists and diaries. We have already noted that it is relatively easy to use short video recordings. The future of teacher education is very likely to involve more extensive use of video (Mann 2016); where this is not feasible, audio recordings may be used.

STIMULATED RECALL

Stimulated recall involves teachers making a short recording of their teaching, then, during playback, identifying a puzzle, issue, or **critical incident** and discussing it with a colleague (see, for example, Lyle 2003). The advantage of this procedure is that it allows teachers to share and comment on their teaching together; it is a springboard for dialogic reflection.

Extract 7.4 is an example of stimulated recall. The teacher, Mary, is explaining how she clarified a piece of vocabulary that she had just elicited. The classroom interaction is presented on the left, with Mary's commentary on the right.

EXTRACT 7.4

[The teacher (T) is eliciting vocabulary items and collecting them on the board. A student (L1) is trying to explain a word.]

Classroom interaction	Teacher's commentary
L1: discographics	*I was going to say it's a false friend but I*
T: ooh what do you mean?	*decided not to because I thought that*
L1: the people who not the people	*might confuse her . . . maybe I*
the (4) the business about music	*misunderstood her now when I look*
record series and	*back at it . . . I understood at the time*
T: is this a word you're thinking of in	*that she meant that this was a*
Basque or Spanish in English I don't	*particular industry but maybe she*
know this word 'disco-graphics' what	*meant a business . . . but I wasn't*
I would say is er (writes on board) like	*prepared to spend a long time on that*
you said 'the music business'	*because it didn't seem important even*
L1: the music business? what is the name	*though there was still a doubt in my*
of of er industry?	*mind . . .*
T: the music industry as well it's	
actually better	

(Walsh 2011)

Mary's self-reflections and insights offer a detailed analysis of a repair strategy that may have backfired and caused added confusion. She is able to rationalise the process and take stock of the different courses of action followed and alternatives rejected ('I was going to say it's a false friend but I decided not to because I thought that might confuse her'). Mary is also able to accept that she may have misunderstood L1's explanation and that she possibly could have allowed more time she had some uncertainty about the outcome of this repair being successful. There is doubt in Mary's comments ('there was still a doubt in my mind . . . '), and in the questions asked by L1 ('the music business? what is the name of . . . industry?').

Stimulated recall is a particularly useful data-led reflective tool, offering as it does an opportunity for teachers to use data to inform their reflections and engage in dialogue to fine-tune their thinking. Even without the transcripts, much can be learnt by participants, and it is a methodology that brings together the various elements necessary for RP to work effectively: tools, data, and dialogue. Stimulated recall is relatively easy to organise, inexpensive, and unobtrusive and has considerable potential for influencing professional development.

ENHANCING SETT: SETTVEO

In Chapter 6, we presented an example of a tool for reflection, the SETT framework, which was designed in collaboration with a group of university TESOL teachers and used to help teachers gain closer understandings of the complex relationship between language, interaction, and learning. SETT consists of four micro-contexts (called *modes*: *managerial, classroom context, materials*, and *skills and systems*) and 14 interactional features (see Chapter 6).

More recently, the framework has been developed as an app, Self Evaluation of Teacher Talk through Video Enhanced Observation (**SETTVEO**). The VEO app was developed by teacher educators Jon Haines and Paul Miller at Newcastle University, UK (see https://veo.co.uk). The app allows users to record and tag videos which can be uploaded to a portal and shared. Using the modes and interactures (interactional features such as display question, teacher echo, etc.) from SETT, SETTVEO allows teachers to classify features of their teaching and reflect on their use. The app can be used in real time (synchronously) or, preferably, once the recording has been made (asynchronously). Figure 7.4 shows a SETTVEO screenshot.

Eight of the SETT interactures appear as tags; the teacher using the app simply plays back a short video and clicks on the appropriate interacture when it occurs. This then appears on the screen as a timestamp. It is possible, during playback, to skip from one feature to the next or to focus on all the occurrences of one interactional feature. So, for example, the user can focus on each occurrence of a display question or, alternatively, simply go from one feature to the next in the order in which they occurred.

One advantage of the app is that it allows teachers to build up a profile of their teaching over time, highlighting which aspects of their teaching could be improved and learning from those which seem to work well. The recordings and reflective comments can be shared online with other users, establishing a professional learning community, which can then be used to foster shared practice, dialogic reflection, and improved levels of professional development.

The VEO concept has been used across the globe for various purposes, including improving initial teacher education in the

Figure 7.4 The SETTVEO interface.
Source: © Paul Miller and Jon Haines.

United Kingdom and Finland; enabling CPD in the United States, China, and Ghana; researching university-level medical education; and evaluating pupil understanding of taught concepts. The advantages that VEO brings to analysing complex situations make it appropriate for studying interaction, where multiple perspectives are possible (for further details, see Seedhouse 2022; Walsh 2019).

RP can be refocused, away from an approach which is individual, involving written reflection, towards one which highlights practices that are data-led, collaborative, and dialogic, using appropriate tools. By adopting a more dialogic, data-led approach to RP, there is greater potential for improving CIC and making teaching and learning more engaged.

This chapter has ended with a technological enhancement of ELTE. It is to the general field of technology in ELT that we turn in the final chapter of this book.

NOTE

1 www.teachingenglish.org.uk/formal-qualifications.

FURTHER READING

Farrell, T.S.C. 2016. *From Trainee to Teacher: Reflective Practice for Novice Teachers.* **London: Equinox.**
This is an introduction to becoming a reflective practitioner and making reflection part of a teacher's professional life. The book has examples of how to do reflection and how to build the process into a teacher's busy life. It contains practical ideas.

Hobbs, V. 2013. 'A Basic Starter Pack': The TESOL Certificate as a Course in Survival. *English Language Teaching Journal* **67 (2): 163–174.**
This paper offers a research-based critical evaluation of initial teacher education courses, specifically the TESOL Certificate offered by Trinity. The paper provides insights into the claims made by course providers and the evaluative comments of trainee teachers.

Mann, S. & Walsh, S. 2017. *Reflective Practice in English Language Teaching. Research-based Principles and Practices.* **Abingdon, Oxon and New York: Routledge.**
This book offers a data-led, evidence-based approach to reflective practice, using examples and vignettes which demonstrate how reflection works in practice. It

highlights the value of dialogue in reflection and suggests practical ways of using reflective tools for professional development.

Walsh, S. and Mann, S. 2019. *The Routledge Handbook of English Language Teacher Education*. Abingdon, Oxon and New York: Routledge. This handbook brings together current thinking about ELTE in a range of international contexts. The chapters are organised thematically. Common constructs, such as reflection and reflexivity, technology, and criticality, are dealt with. The book makes extensive use of data and the voices of other practitioners.

8

TECHNOLOGY IN AND
OUT OF THE CLASSROOM

OUT WITH THE OLD, IN WITH THE NEW

Technology has supported language learning for centuries: the invention of printing, the advent of audio recording and broadcasting, photography, cinema, TV, language laboratories, and computers all have played their part. In our time, computers and the internet have led the way.

In this final chapter, we look at technology in ELT. This theme could occupy a whole book rather than one chapter, and relevant books are listed under 'Further Reading'. But because technology is constantly changing, with a new array of technical affordances launched almost daily, relegating existing technologies to the dustbin, we restrict the scope of this chapter; any new technologies lauded may well be out of date by the time you read this book.

CORPORA

LOOKING AT LANGUAGE

One development at the end of the twentieth century which impacted ELT was technology which facilitated the storage, searchability, and retrievability of massive amounts of text in the form of corpora. With a corpus, linguists could get a more objective picture of how language is used by groups of users, such as national corpora like the BNC (British), AusNC (Australian), and ANC (American) national corpora,[1] as well as corpora

DOI: 10.4324/9781003350316-8

of world Englishes, such as the International Corpus of English (ICE),[2] specialised corpora (e.g., business or academic corpora), and sociolinguistic corpora like the Corpus of London Teenage English (COLT) or the Oxford Children's Corpus. Additionally, **learner corpora**, compiled from learners' writing and speaking, have enabled researchers to obtain objective evidence of learner development (Granger et al. 2015; Römer and Garner 2022). One example of specialised data collection particularly relevant to themes discussed in Chapter 3 is Kieran Harrington's corpus of spoken interactions among asylum seekers at a reception centre in Ireland. The residents come from varied L1 backgrounds and communicate effectively with one another using what little English they possess. These are not L2 English users in the classroom or learners writing essays; rather, it is a corpus *in the wild*, a valuable resource for understanding ESL contexts of use (Harrington 2022).

Research into corpora has enabled the production of dictionaries, reference and pedagogical grammars, coursebooks, and supplementary materials, all of which are now well established in the ELT marketplace. For teachers, free, online resources, such as dictionaries and grammar references, the English Vocabulary Profile, and the English Grammar Profile (see Chapter 3) and, for EAP, the Oxford Phrasal Academic Lexicon (OPAL), are all easy to access through major search engines. Initially, when corpora first came to the notice of English language teachers, there was some hesitance and misunderstanding as to what this would mean for teachers' day-to-day work. However, using corpus-informed materials needs no computer skills – all the technical work is done before the corpus statistics and data are incorporated into the materials.

Incorporating corpus evidence into ELT materials was not without controversy and difficulties in the early days (for example, debates around authenticity – see Chapter 4), but corpora are here to stay. O'Keeffe et al. (2007) look at the many ways that corpora can be exploited in ELT. Corpora containing multimodal data (audio, transcript, and video) will become increasingly available as technology improves. The *Routledge Handbook of Corpus Linguistics* (O'Keeffe and McCarthy 2022) contains chapters by renowned experts on every aspect of corpora and their applications.

CORPORA, TEACHERS, AND LEARNERS

For the most part, corpora have been used by linguists and, latterly, material writers. However, user-friendly software and open access to corpora have meant that teachers can do their own research into language use. *Google Ngram Viewer*,[3] for example, enables quick searches of huge numbers of books for words and phrases, and easy comparisons can be made between synonyms and between British and American English and how frequency of use changes over time.

Many scholars advocate the use of corpus data directly with learners through **data-driven learning (DDL)** (Chambers 2022). In this approach, learners are typically shown a **concordance** (a screen or printout of a word or phrase showing it in use with surrounding co-text) and read it to notice patterns or to work out meanings of a key item. Figure 8.1 shows sample concordance lines for the word *corner* from the OANC spoken texts. Observing the different preposition patterns is a typical DDL task:

- *On* is used for building locations.
- *In* is used with parts of US states (*Rhode Island, Colorado*).
- *Around* is used to pinpoint one location relative to another.

been and uh because we live on a corner and back up to a real uh
a fenced in backyard we're on a corner and we look out at a creek
the street and there's one on every corner this is true this is very true
was buildings going up on every corner every week and yes and and
right up in the uh in the northeast corner of Rhode Island and and the
a waterfall and a little pond in one corner i mean that was like the most
we lived in the southwestern corner of the state so we could go to
one year we went to the southwest corner of Colorado into Durango and
can at any high school or any street corner they tell me but i don't know
i i'd go with the ones on the street corner because people are thinking
somebody's apartment around the corner i said see this is it hm time to
parks that are down around the corner from here and you know it's
parents, who, again, live around the corner from Mr. Speckman. They
new uh news rack right around the corner from where i live which
piano teacher lived right around the corner and the dance teacher was all

Figure 8.1 Sample concordance lines for *corner* (OANC).

This exercise is easy enough for the trained eye. However, learners may experience difficulties or distractions, including:

- Low-frequency words (*creek, rack, pond*).
- Spoken grammar (*was buildings*).
- Insufficient context in some lines.
- Having to read 'vertically' and 'right to left' to capture the patterns.

Training in what a corpus provides and how to interpret concordances is a necessary preliminary to DDL; editing of raw concordances may also be needed.

DDL has been used primarily in higher education (HE) contexts. Pascual Pérez-Paredes, in a major survey, concludes:

> DDL normalisation in language education has only taken place in a limited number of contexts where language teachers and DDL researchers subsume the same roles in HE, particularly in Asia, Europe and the US.
>
> (2022: 53)

DDL is probably best suited to more advanced proficiency levels. Its value rests on the potential for developing language awareness and noticing (Hadley 2002) and the feeling it may give of authentic encounters with L2 (see Gilquin and Granger 2022). At the time of writing, the jury is out on its effectivity compared with traditional methods, though promising results have been reported (e.g., Boulton 2009).

ELT ONLINE

Advances in video-conference software (VCS) and the Covid pandemic caused an explosion in online working practices (Stickler 2022). The pandemic led to a suspension of face-to-face (F2F) classes globally (Bozkurt et al. 2020). Teachers were forced to find alternative working practices – radically different ways of interacting with and teaching their students. Advances in technology enabled language teachers to use VCS in **synchronous online lessons** (**SOLs**). These bring teacher and students together in a virtual online space. Participants can see and hear each other, discuss and share ideas, and view and use teaching materials. In one sense, SOLs are similar to the F2F classroom; they involve a teacher, students, materials, lesson aims, time limits, and interaction. However, the dialogic triangle on page 104 has to be modified to allow for a fourth mediating participant – the technology (Figure 8.2).

Teaching online calls for a range of different skills to teaching F2F. Classroom practices look and feel different and take place in a two-dimensional space (Figure 8.3). The SOL has to engage and

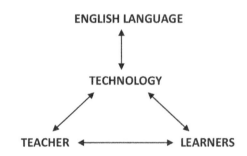

Figure 8.2 The communication triangle modified.

Figure 8.3 A SOL.

involve learners using only camera and microphone, maximise and maintain interaction in a virtual classroom, deal with technical glitches, and support students in their use of technology (Rehn et al. 2018). The differences between F2F teaching and SOLs far outweigh the similarities (see Carrier et al. 2017).

SOLs have a number of affordances: for example, they permit language learning to take place even when F2F teaching is not possible. They also suffer constraints, including:

- Physical locations and time zones may be different.
- Teacher and students are not always able to see one other easily (there may be a policy of 'cameras off' which restricts interaction, badly angled cameras, muted microphones, etc.).
- Vital communicative cues are often missed, such as a raised eyebrow, eye contact, head nods, frowns.
- In SOLs, feedback is less obvious, frequently reduced, or absent. Feedback ensures everyone is 'on the same page'.
- Technology failures, class management issues, difficulties in audibility, and comprehension are not uncommon.

There may also be environmental distractions making it harder for students to engage (Peachey 2017). The challenges of SOLs may limit a teacher's ability to promote interaction and create 'space for learning' (Walsh and Li 2013). As Moorhouse says:

> The VCS sessions are still more 'bumpy' and more teacher-centred than face-to-face sessions. Group and whole class discussions are characterised by longer silences and shorter student responses.
>
> (2020: 2)

Similarly, Payne comments that 'conversational turn-taking in a video conference is challenging enough when everyone is speaking their first language (L1), let alone an L2' (2020: 246).

To overcome the challenges, a range of teaching strategies have been suggested to enhance interaction online:

- *Breakout rooms*, available on certain VCS platforms. These allow students to work in small groups independently of the teacher.
- Different *modes* of interaction, such as chat, student polls, and 'drawing' (Kohnke and Moorhouse 2020).

- Time at the beginning and end of a lesson for participants to have social conversations.
- Other types of technology support (e.g., messaging services) to ensure there is a way of getting back to a lesson when there is a technical breakdown.
- Time at the beginning of a course explaining the technology, outlining different modes of interaction, and suggesting working practices.

In a recent survey by Moorhouse et al. (2021), researchers set out to identify which competencies are needed by teachers in synchronous online teaching. Using the CIC construct, the team identified three additional competencies teachers need when working online; collectively these competencies constitute **e-CIC** (electronically mediated classroom interactional competence). The three are technological, management, and teacher interactional competencies.

TECHNOLOGICAL COMPETENCIES

In the Moorhouse et al. study, teachers pinpointed the need for a high level of technological competence when using VCS. They commented on the need to feel comfortable with the technology and to find ways of combining VCS with other tools, such as game-based and learning management platforms.

MANAGEMENT COMPETENCIES

Classroom management contributes to teacher efficacy in F2F contexts (see, for example, Buchanan and Timmis 2019). In online teaching, the management of learning is even more crucial because many features of F2F interaction are missing. Online classroom management may include:

- Exploiting the chat function when giving an instruction or explanation.
- Screen-sharing a lesson plan.
- Using the 'virtual flipped classroom' (Abdullah et al. 2019): students watch a video out of class for discussion in class.
- Ensuring students understand an activity before going into breakout rooms.

- Allowing students to choose how they respond, whether through chat or audio.

TEACHER INTERACTIONAL COMPETENCIES

Some of the online challenges for teachers require specific interactional competences:

- Using different modes of VCS: whole class together, breakout rooms, chat, audio, polls, and so on.
- Extending wait time, allowing students more time to respond or complete a task.
- Developing a range of questioning techniques appropriate to SOLs.
- Adopting a different IRF exchange structure. Instead of the F2F model, the Moorhouse et al. 2021 study suggests:

  I: closed question to whole class
  R: students respond using chat
  F: a more open question to one or more students
  R: students respond using microphone
  F: teacher offers evaluation

- Providing more opportunities for **rehearsal,** involving students working privately or in small groups before giving a response in plenary.

Another suggestion is for teachers to consider how students already engage in online activity (e.g., social media, gaming, web searches) and harness these experiences in the classroom (Hafner 2019). By involving students in creating an online space for learning, there is potential in producing SOLs which are effective and where students feel motivated.

TAMING THE WILDERNESS

MOBILE LEARNING

In this book, we have referred to English language learning that takes place informally outside of institutional contexts as learning *in the wild*. Learners worldwide encounter L2 English in popular culture and media and have access to that world quite literally in the palm of their hand through phones, tablets, and e-readers. Such devices combine tools which a couple of decades ago would have meant carrying a separate camera, audio recorder, dictionary, reference work, portable radio, telephone, diary, notebook, timepiece, and so on. Learning English as an L2 can therefore be enhanced through **mobile learning**. Gavin Dudeney and Nicky Hockly say:

> Mobile devices are not just mobile in the sense of 'portable'. They can make the learning experience itself mobile if the teacher is able to design pedagogically sound and imaginative communicative tasks that take the learning experience beyond the classroom walls.
>
> (2016: 219)

But the e-world is a wilderness. Appropriate management of mobile learning, or **mobile assisted language learning** (**MALL**), combines the virtual language lesson with learning in the wild. Dudeney and Hockly provide an example of a MALL project carried out with CEFR A1 and B1 learners using their phones (2016: 226–227). Smartphones also typically offer immediate access to translation apps. If used strategically (as we saw in Elena's case in Chapter 3) and in appropriate circumstances, these can be extremely useful and educative and can also be a resource for MALL.

SCREENING MATERIALS

Robert Vanderplank, surveying the use of audio-visual resources in language teaching in 2010, commented that TV and language laboratories had survived well alongside internet-based developments (2010). Although the traditional, drill-based language lab may be under threat, the role of audio-visual media in language learning has persisted and grown in the last decade. Video hosting sites have become globally popular, with videos often attracting millions of viewers, and ELT videos abound. These include an unregulated, huge number of short videos purporting to teach English grammar for learners. At the time of writing, for example, several online videos offering tuition in English modal verbs have been viewed more than a million times. This is a double-edged sword. On the one hand, many of the videos are colourful, sparky, informative, and entertaining; on the other hand, it is often difficult or impossible to establish the credentials of the person delivering the tuition. Sadly, it is not difficult to find videos that make patently muddle-headed statements about English usage. Trustworthy sites for EFL/ESL video tuition include the British Council's Learn English channel[4] and TESOL International,[5] which has videos for teachers giving tips on teaching language and skills in its Interest Section webinars.

> ### RESEARCH EVIDENCE
>
> Research suggests that learners watching online videos not necessarily created for language learning benefit from the multimedia affordances of subtitles, on-screen texts, and audio and visual supports to comprehension, as well as experiencing authentic L2 encounters and acquiring language along the way (e.g., Tolson 2010; Arndt and Woore 2018; Alobaid 2020).

It can be difficult for learners to assess the value of online videos and blogs for their language learning. From a teacher's viewpoint, the most important task is 'screening' (in both senses of viewing *and* evaluating) online videos and blogs before directing students towards them. Online materials of this kind lend themselves to use in **blended learning** (where classroom and online learning both form part of a course; see the papers in McCarthy 2016b) and the **flipped classroom**, where some uses of materials are transferred out of the classroom to the online environment, releasing classroom time for more collaborative face-to-face interaction (Turan and Akdag-Cimen 2020). The teacher can facilitate the process by pre-online tasks to prepare students before they watch/read the online material. In this way, learning in the wild becomes less 'untamed' and less open in an unsupported way to the wilderness of the online landscape.

LET THE MACHINE DECIDE?

AUTOMATED ASSESSMENT

ELT involves frequent testing in the form of quizzes and classroom tests, national exams, and high-stakes international tests. Educational assessment is a discipline in itself; in this book, we keep to matters more directly related to teaching and learning. Standard, major works on language assessment provide all the necessary information on how tests are constructed and interpreted. *The Routledge Handbook of Language Testing* (Fulcher and Harding 2022) covers every aspect, with chapters by world experts.

A distinction exists between summative and formative assessment. **Summative assessment** tests the learner's achieved proficiency at a certain point (e.g., an international exam); **formative assessment** concerns the learner's ongoing development and points to the future, integrating the understandings it provides with teaching and learning. It is assessment *for* learning.

Technology is increasingly involved in both kinds of assessment, with computers playing a role in the delivery and scoring of major examinations (Saville 2017), but it is in formative assessment that technology comes fully into its own. Automated feedback on EFL/ESL student writing is well advanced, with automated assessment of speaking not far behind. Learners input their writing or speaking to an app and receive performance scores but can also receive **adaptive feedback**: the machine recommends future courses of action based on current and past performance. The machine can 'judge' performance because it has been trained on learner and native-user data and refines its feedback based on ever-growing volumes of incoming data from new and existing users. The work of the Automated Language Testing and Assessment (ALTA) team at the University of Cambridge, UK (http://alta.cambridgeenglish.org), is at the forefront of such developments.[6] In a different way, Xiaofei Lu has shown how computational analysis of learner essays at the advanced level can detect indices of syntactic complexity (2010).

INTERACTION AND THE BOT

The growth of artificial intelligence (AI) has raised the possibility of communicating with machines and receiving verbal feedback at a quasi-human level from a chatbot. **Chatbots** work autonomously and, once trained, theoretically need no further human intervention, refining themselves constantly based on incoming data. Chatbots can be either text based or voice based. Smart speakers for home use which respond to commands to carry out tasks and fulfil requests for information are already commonplace, and applications in ELT and education in general are growing. Not least of the controversies surrounding bots is their ability to generate authentic-looking texts (e.g., student essays) on command that can fool all but the trained eye. An article in *New Scientist* magazine in 2023 looked at the incorporation of AI chatbots into search engines, noting that the engine will be able to respond to a request for a text on a subject and write it as a Shakespearean sonnet, write a job application for you, or automate blogs (Sparkes 2023). However, the same magazine also reminded its readers that chatbots were just calculating machines which simply predict 'the most likely subsequent word in a sequence based on all the relationships of words they have seen' (Wilkins 2023).

The Cambridge University ALTA team, at the time of writing, have developed a chatbot for learners of English which simulates conversations on common, everyday topics. Its creators (Tyen et al. 2022a, 2022b) have based its adaptivity on a modified version of the English Vocabulary Profile (EVP; see Chapter 3), which enables the chatbot to communicate at an appropriate CEFR level with its human interlocutor. However, since the EVP has only a restricted vocabulary, the machine was also trained to appropriately grade words outside of the EVP list. The team aimed to 'generate outputs that are of the appropriate difficulty level in terms of structure, content, as well as choice of words' (Tyen et al. 2022a: 237), reflecting the complexity vertex of the complexity-accuracy-fluency triangle we have frequently referred to in this book.

The advantages of the chatbot are that it gives learners opportunities to practise under less stressful conditions than in real-life conversation or in the 'exposed' environment of the classroom, as well as offering individual access at a time and at a pace to suit the user and greater opportunities to explore topics of personal interest and more speaking time than is the case in the busy, time-constrained EFL/ESL classroom.

RESEARCH EVIDENCE

Promising results have been obtained on the use of chatbots in EFL contexts. A project in South Korea involved more than 300 EFL students from 10–15 years old engaging in verbal interaction with the machine on a variety of tasks (e.g., ordering restaurant food). Students generally felt comfortable talking to the chatbot and felt it helped improve their speaking skills but remained aware that it was not like talking to a human (Yang et al. 2022).

Tyen et al. (2022b) list four human-like qualities the chatbot should aspire to recreate:

- A 'personality' – a sense in which the human user can attribute individuality and character to the machine's output.
- Knowledge – the ability to search and retrieve useful and appropriate information.
- Empathy – like a human interlocutor, knowing what to say when in order to create and maintain interaction.
- A safe environment free from the dangers of interacting with strangers on the web and free from offensive or inappropriate content.

This is a tall order, but AI is already proving its ability to create humanlike features of conversational interaction, and technological advances in AI will undoubtedly lead to the refinement of machines which support language learning. Some of the pros of the chatbot (no-stress environment, individualisation for the learner, working at the learner's pace, etc.) were already a feature of the language laboratories so prevalent in the 1960s and 1970s for listening and drilling of language features. The chatbot is a descendant of that technology but creates a more interactive experience for its users. It is, nonetheless, a machine and is at times capable of churning out nonsense.

In these data from the ALTA chatbot (Extract 8.1), the learner is at approximately B1 level. The learner could also look up dictionary definitions during the chat by clicking on words in a chatbot message. In this case, the learner clicked on *endeavors*; the chatbot typically uses American spelling based on AmE training data.[7] Despite lexicogrammatical infelicities on the part of the learner, the chatbot has responded coherently and the conversation flows.

EXTRACT 8.1

Chatbot: Doctor is the hardest profession to get into, but the most rewarding, in my opinion.

Learner: Yes i agree with you. When I was young i was dreaming myself as a doctor

Chatbot: I have a friend who would like to be an orthopedic surgeon some day.

Learner: I wish he achieve his goal! He will help a lot of people.

Chatbot: I hope so, his passion is what got him into it. Good luck with your endeavors!

Learner: What about you? what you do to bring foor to the table?

Chatbot: Good question! I like to volunteer my time to be honest. It's very therapeutic.

Learner: I think that it's really is! I have never volunteered. I dont know how to start. can you give me any advise?

Chatbot: What kind of things were you thinking about doing? There's so many different types of volunteering opportunities.

(Reproduced by kind permission)

One interesting question is whether the technology will advance to a stage where the so-called *ELIZA effect* (Hofstadter 1995: Preface 4), when humans wrongly believe they are interacting with another human rather than a machine, becomes standard reality. The implications for ELT are considerable, with learners of the future engaging in spoken and written interaction with bots, where classrooms are managed by robots (Figure 8.4) – a world where human teachers

Figure 8.4 The future of ELT?

may become increasingly redundant. In the meantime, learner–chatbot interaction can provide practice which students can engage in fully in the knowledge that they are interacting with a machine.

There is nothing inherently wrong with technological interventions in the language-learning process, and technology has always had a role in education. However, the same basic questions remain: are non-human interactions received by learners as 'authentic' encounters with L2, and can the machine replicate the good teacher's moment-by-moment CIC skill of harnessing learning opportunities and understanding their learners? In other words, can artificially intelligent machines acquire the fifth skill?

THE JOURNEY AHEAD

This book has tried to cover the *basics* of ELT. Inevitably, in a short introduction, some areas of the profession have received a lighter touch. We have focused on aspects of teaching and learning where interaction is paramount. If you are a practising English language teacher, or one about to embark on an ELT career, we hope you will embrace our commitment to the centrality of interaction and carry it with you into the future. You have our best wishes.

NOTES

1 BNC: www.natcorp.ox.ac.uk/; AusNC: www.ausnc.org.au/; ANC: https://anc.org/.
2 http://http://ice-corpora.net.
3 https://books.google.com/ngrams/info.
4 www.youtube.com/@BritishCouncilEnglish.
5 www.youtube.com/@tesolinc.
6 For example, the *Write and Improve* facility at https://writeandimprove.com/.
7 Background information to the extract provided by Gladys Tyen: personal correspondence, 17 March 2021.

FURTHER READING

Carrier, M., Damerow, R. M. and Bailey, K. M. (eds) 2017. *Digital Language Learning and Teaching*. New York: Routledge.

This is a comprehensive collection of chapters on all aspects of digital technology in language learning, covering synchronous and asynchronous online and blended learning, the flipped classroom, and many more topics we have been unable to cover in this chapter.

O'Keeffe, A. and McCarthy, M. J. (eds) 2022. *The Routledge Handbook of Corpus Linguistics.* **Second edition. Abingdon, Oxon: Routledge**.
This handbook covers all aspects of corpus linguistics, from building corpora to investigating language use, language acquisition, and practical applications in language teaching, in 47 chapters written by leading experts in the field.

Stickler, U. 2022. *Technology and Language Teaching.* **Cambridge: Cambridge University Press.**
This short introduction to online teaching covers all the dilemmas involved in the move to online teaching and the challenges teachers have faced by being catapulted into the online world. It focuses on choosing appropriate tools and making online teaching learner centred.

GLOSSARY OF KEY TERMS

assessment
Summative assessment tests learner's achieved proficiency at a certain point (e.g., an international exam); formative assessment is ongoing and provides feedback to teachers and students.

blended learning
Combining in-class and online learning. Some learning takes place online, allowing more time for activities in class.

CEFR
Common European Framework of Reference, consisting of three levels, A, B, and C, each subdivided into A1, A2, B1, B2, C1, and C2. A1 is the lowest level of proficiency and C2 the highest.

CELTA
Certificate in English Language Teaching to Adults – now called Certificate in Teaching English to Speakers of Other Languages).

chunks
Also known as clusters, lexical bundles, or formulaic sequences. Groups of words which combine in a fixed way and have a unitary meaning (*at the end of the day, to be honest*).

classroom interaction
All aspects of classroom life and learning depend on the quality of language used between and among teacher and learners.

classroom management (CM)
CM is concerned with the strategies teachers use to create a comfortable, purposeful learning environment.

CLIL
Content and language integrated learning. School students in non-English-speaking countries may learn school subjects with English as the medium of instruction.

code switching
Changing from one language to another mid-stream. Code switching tends to occur predictably and at certain places in a bilingual speaker's use of their two languages.

communicative language teaching (CLT)
Also known as the communicative approach. Based on the idea that language is for 'doing' and achieving communicative goals.

continuing professional development (CPD)
Teachers develop during their career through experiential learning, action research, and reflective practice.

corpus (plural corpora)
A computerised collection of texts which can be analysed using dedicated software.

curriculum
A statement of the aims and scope of a teaching programme, a high-level way of organising learning (e.g., a national educational curriculum).

data-driven learning (DDL)
The use of corpus data directly with learners to promote noticing and language awareness.

DELTA
Diploma in English Language Teaching to Adults.

dialect
The combinations of accent, grammar, and vocabulary in different geographical regions.

dialogic reflection
Reflecting on your teaching through dialogue with a colleague or critical friend.

direct repair
Error correction done quickly, using minimal interruptions to maintain the flow of a lesson.

discourse
Texts in context, which are typically longer than a single sentence. The study of discourse is discourse analysis.

display questions
Questions asked by teachers to get student to 'display' what they know. Teachers already know the answer to their questions.

elicitation
Asking questions to generate responses.

ELTE
English Language Teacher Education.

EMI
English as the medium of instruction.

English as a lingua franca
Use of English to communicate when no individual taking part in the discourse may be a native user.

English for academic purposes (EAP)
The special uses of English which underpin academic subjects.

extensive reading
Reading on broad topics of interest often done for enjoyment.

feedback
Another term for *error correction*. **Scaffolded feedback** involves the teacher discussing the error with the learner, encouraging self-correction.

fluency
A perception of language 'flowing'. Fluency entails putting meanings into words coherently, automatically, and without hesitation.

genres
Text types which have evolved over time, such as novels, academic dissertations, newspaper editorials, and so on.

grammar
The set of conventions that govern how phrases, clauses, and (in writing) sentences are put together.

illocutionary force
A speaker's intended meaning, which may or may not be reflected in the words spoken.

inference
Reading or listening between the lines: working out meaning where it is not directly stated or where the language is unfamiliar.

information gap activities
These work on the principle that participants share some, but not all, the information on a given topic and interact to share everything.

input hypothesis
The idea that L2 acquisition takes place when learners receive input they can understand but which includes some language that is new.

intensive reading
Reading in detail using bottom-up processing.

interactional competence
Sometimes referred to as the 'fifth skill'. Refers to the ability to co-construct meaning through interaction.

IRF
Classroom discourse typically follows this pattern: teacher initiates (I) by asking a question; students respond (R), and teachers give feedback (F).

learner corpora
Data compiled from learners' writing and speaking,

lexis
All the words and expressions of English together form the lexis (vocabulary).

listenership
The ability to understand, acknowledge, engage with, and respond to incoming talk.

lockstep
The whole class working together as one rather than individually, in pairs or in groups.

mental lexicon
Vocabulary stored in memory; the 'storehouse' is referred to as the mental lexicon.

methodology
The study of systematic ways of doing things.

mobile assisted language learning (MALL)
MALL combines the virtual language lesson with learning in the wild using mobile devices.

morphemes
The smallest units of meaning. A word must contain at least one morpheme.

motivation
Personal attitudes which drive learning, for example, willingness to put effort into learning, goal orientation, a feeling of enjoyment of learning.

phonemes
Sets of sounds which are the basis of meaningful communication in any given language.

phonetics
The study of human sounds.

phonology
The study of how sounds combine into regular patterns and form a system.

plurilingualism
The idea that teachers and learners can exploit their knowledge of languages and intercultural awareness in the teaching/learning process.

PPP (presentation-practice-production)
A popular language teaching method where new language is presented, then drilled, before learners are given opportunities to use it freely.

pragmatics
The study of meaning in context.

PRESET
Pre-service teacher education.

referential questions
Referential questions often begin with a *wh-* question such as *who, why, what, when, where,* or *which* in order to generate a more conversational kind of interaction.

reflective practice (RP)
Thinking about your teaching, evaluating what you do, and making changes to improve your practice.

scaffolding
The linguistic support given to a learner, for example, a teacher might 'feed in' a specific word to help learners with a task. Scaffolding involves challenge to maintain interest and involvement and support to ensure understanding.

schema (plural schemata)
Schemata are mental representations of phenomena and events, based on real-world knowledge, cultural background, and experience.

second language acquisition (SLA)
The study of how second languages are acquired.

Self-Evaluation of Teacher Talk (SETT)
The SETT framework comprises four classroom micro-contexts (called **modes**) and 13 interactional features (called **interactures**).

semantics
The study of meaning.

socio-cultural theory (SCT)
Emphasises learning as a social process. Learning takes place as learners interact with the 'expert' teacher, or each other.

speech act theory
The theory that all utterances perform acts such as requesting, explaining, complimenting, apologising, giving permission, and so on.

STEM
Science, technology, engineering, and maths.

stimulated recall
Teachers make a short recording of their teaching and analyse it to identify a question which they discuss with a colleague.

syllabus
A document that describes what the contents of a language course will be and the order in which the content will be taught.

synchronous online lessons (SOLs)
SOLs bring teacher and students together in a virtual online space. Participants can see and hear each other, discuss and share ideas, and view and use teaching materials.

syntax
The system of how structures are organised into sentences.

task-based learning (TBL)
TBL involves the specification not of a sequence of language forms but a sequence of communicative tasks to be carried out in the target language.

TESOL
Teaching English to Speakers of Other Languages.

translanguaging
Translanguaging occurs when speakers draw on their repertoire of whatever language(s) they know, going from one to another in strategic decisions to facilitate communication.

universal grammar
The underlying principles of organisation that all languages share.

vocabulary

Another term for the lexis of a language. **Depth** of vocabulary (all the things we know about a word) is as important as **breadth** (how many words we know).

zone of proximal development (ZPD)

A theoretical space which exists between a learner and an expert (such as a teacher); learners develop in this space by interacting with the expert teacher.

REFERENCES

Abdullah, M. Y., Hussin, S. and Ismail, K. 2019. Implementation of Flipped Classroom Model and Its Effectiveness on English Speaking Performance. *International Journal of Emerging Technologies in Learning* 14: 130–147.

Alobaid, A. 2020. Smart Multimedia Learning of ICT: Role and Impact on Language Learners' Writing Fluency – YouTube Online English Learning Resources as an Example. *Smart Learning Environments* 7 (24). Online at https://doi.org/10.1186/s40561-020-00134-7.

Anderson, J. 2015. Affordance, Learning Opportunities and the Lesson Plan Proforma. *ELT Journal* 69 (3): 228–238.

Anderson, N. J. 2014. Developing Engaged Second Language Readers. In M. Celce-Murcia, D. M. Brinton and M. A. Snow (eds), *Teaching English as a Second or Foreign Language*. Fourth edition. Boston, MA: Heinle Cengage Learning/National Geographic Leaning, 170–188.

Arndt, H. and Woore, R. 2018. Vocabulary Learning from Watching YouTube Videos and Reading Blog Posts. *Language Learning and Technology* 22 (3): 124–142.

Baguley, N. 2019. Supporting Newly Qualified Teachers. In S. Walsh and S. Mann (eds), *The Routledge Handbook of English Language Teacher Education*. Abingdon, Oxon: Routledge, 125–137.

Bakeer, S. 2023. *Discourse Markers in Doctoral Supervision*. Abingdon, Oxon: Routledge.

Bakhtin, M. 1981. Discourse in the Novel. In M. Holquist (ed.), *The Dialogic Imagination: Four Essays by M. M. Bakhtin*. Austin: University of Texas Press, 259–422.

Bax, S. 2003. The End of CLT? A Context Approach to Language Teaching. *ELT Journal* 57 (3): 278–287.

Bell, A. 1984. Language Style as Audience Design. *Language in Society* 13 (2): 145–204.

Benwell, B. and Stokoe, E. 2006. *Discourse and Identity*. Edinburgh: Edinburgh University Press.

Berlitz 1966. *English First Book*. Paris: Societé Internationale des Écoles Berlitz.

Bland, J. 2015. Introduction. In J. Bland (ed.), *Teaching English to Young Learners*. London: Bloomsbury Academic, 1–12.

Bleistein, T. and Lewis, M. 2015. *One-on-One Language Teaching and Learning*. Basingstoke, Hants: Palgrave Macmillan.

Bohlke, D. 2014. Fluency-Oriented Second Language Teaching. In M. Celce-Murcia, D. M. Brinton and M. A. Snow (eds), *Teaching English as a Second or Foreign Language*. Fourth edition. Boston, MA: Heinle Cengage Learning/National Geographic Leaning, 121–135.

Boud, D., Keogh, R. and Walker, D. 1985. What Is Reflection in Learning? In D. Boud, R. Keogh and D. Walker (eds), *Reflection: Turning Experience into Learning*. London: Kogan Page Ltd, 7–17.

Boulton, A. 2009. Testing the Limits of Data-Driven Learning: Language Proficiency and Training. *ReCALL* 21 (1): 37–54.

Bozkurt, A., Jung, I., Xiao, J., et al. 2020. A Global Outlook to the Interruption of Education Due to COVID-19 Pandemic: Navigating in a Time of Uncertainty and Crisis. *Asian Journal of Distance Education* 15 (1): 1–126.

Braine, G. 2018. Non-Native-Speaker English Teachers. In C. A. Chapelle (ed.), *The Encyclopedia of Applied Linguistics*. online at *Wiley Online Library*: https://doi.org/10.1002/9781405198431.wbeal0871.pub2.

Brazil, D. 1997. *The Communicative Value of Intonation in English*. Cambridge: Cambridge University Press.

Breen, M. 1987. Contemporary Paradigms in Syllabus Design Part II. *Language Teaching* 20 (3): 157–174.

Breen, M. 1998. Navigating the Discourse: On What Is Learned in the Language Classroom. In W. A. Renandya and G. M. Jacobs (eds), *Learners and Language Learning: Anthology Series 39*. Singapore: SEAMO Regional Language Centre, 115–144.

Brinton, D. 2014. Tools and Techniques of Effective Second/Foreign Language Teaching. In M. Celce-Murcia, D. M. Brinton and M. A. Snow (eds), *Teaching English as a Second or Foreign Language*. Fourth edition. Boston, MA: Heinle Cengage Learning/National Geographic Leaning, 340–361.

British Council 2013. *The English Effect*. Published online and downloadable at www.britishcouncil.org/research-policy-insight/policy-reports/the-english-effect.

British Council 2015. *Continuing Professional Development Framework for Teachers*. Published online and downloadable at www.teachingenglish.org.uk/publications/resource-books/british-council-cpd-framework.

Bruner, J. 1990. *Acts of Meaning*. Cambridge, MA: Harvard University Press.

Buchanan, H. and Timmis, I. 2019. Classroom Management: Art, Craft or Science? In S. Walsh and S. Mann (eds), *The Routledge Handbook of English Language Teacher Education*. Abingdon, Oxon: Routledge, 319–334.

Buck, G. 2001. *Assessing Listening*. Cambridge: Cambridge University Press.

Burns, A. and Roberts, C. 2010. Migration and Adult Language Learning: Global Flows and Local Transpositions. *TESOL Quarterly* 44 (3): 409–419.

Burton, G. 2022a. What Can a Corpus Tell Us about Grammar Teaching Materials? In A. O'Keeffe and M. J. McCarthy (eds), *The Routledge Handbook of Corpus Linguistics*. Second edition. Abingdon, Oxon: Routledge, 358–370.

Burton, G. 2022b. Selecting Language for Materials Writing. In J. Norton and H. Buchanan (eds), *The Routledge Handbook of Materials Development for Language Teaching*. Abingdon, Oxon: Routledge, 78–92.

Canagarajah, A. S. 1999. Interrogating the 'Native Speaker Fallacy': Non-Linguistic Roots, Non-Pedagogical Results. In G. Braine (ed.), *Non-Native Educators in English Language Teaching*. Mahwah, NJ: Erlbaum 77–92.

Candlin, C. N. 1987. Towards Task-Based Language Learning. In C. N. Candlin and D. Murphy (eds), *Language Learning Tasks*. London: Prentice Hall, 5–22.

Capel, A. 2015. The English Vocabulary Profile. In J. Harrison and F. Barker (eds), *English Profile in Practice*. Cambridge: Cambridge University Press, 9–27.

Carrier, M., Damerow, R. M. and Bailey, K. M. (eds) 2017. *Digital Language Learning and Teaching*. New York: Routledge.

Carter, R. and McCarthy, M. J. 1995. Grammar and the Spoken Language. *Applied Linguistics* 16 (2): 141–158.

Carter, R. and McCarthy, M. J. 1997. *Exploring Spoken English*. Cambridge: Cambridge University Press.

Carter, R. and McCarthy, M. J. 2017. Spoken Grammar: Where Are We and Where Are We Going? *Applied Linguistics* 3 (1): 1–20.

Cenoz, J., Genesee, F. and Gorter, D. 2014. Critical Analysis of CLIL: Taking Stock and Looking Forward. *Applied Linguistics* 35 (3): 243–262.

Chambers, A. 2022. What Is Data-Driven Learning? In A. O'Keeffe and M. J. McCarthy (eds), *The Routledge Handbook of Corpus Linguistics*. Second edition. Abingdon, Oxon: Routledge, 416–429.

Chiswick, B. R. and Miller, P. W. 2003. The Complementarity of Language and Other Human Capital: Immigrant Earnings in Canada. *Economics of Education Review* 22: 469–480.

Chiswick, B. R. and Miller, P. W. 2015. International Migration and the Economics of Language. In B. R. Chiswick and P. W. Miller (eds), *Handbook of the Economics of International Migration, Volume 1A*. Oxford: Elsevier, 211–269.

Chomsky, N. 1959. Review of *Verbal Behavior* by B. F. Skinner. *Language* 35 (1): 26–58.

Collier, V. P. 1987. Age and Rate of Acquisition of Second Language for Academic Purposes. *TESOL Quarterly* 21 (4): 617–641.

Cook, V. 1999. Going beyond the Native Speaker in Language Teaching. *TESOL Quarterly* 33 (2): 185–209.

Cook, V. 2016. Where Is the Native Speaker Now? *TESOL Quarterly* 50 (1): 186–189.

Copland, F. 2012. Legitimate Talk in Feedback Conferences. *Applied Linguistics* 33 (1): 1–20.

Council of Europe 2001. *Common European Framework of Reference for Languages: Learning, Teaching, Assessment.* Cambridge: Cambridge University Press.

Council of Europe 2020. *Common European Framework of Reference for Languages: Learning, Teaching, Assessment – Companion Volume.* Strasbourg: Council of Europe Publishing. Online at www.coe.int/lang-cefr.

Coyle, D., Hood, P. and Marsh, D. 2010. *CLIL: Content and Language Integrated Learning.* Cambridge: Cambridge University Press.

Crystal, D. 2018. Regional Variation. In *The Cambridge Encyclopedia of the English Language.* Cambridge: Cambridge University Press, 318–385.

Cummins, J. 1981. Age on Arrival and Immigrant Second Language Learning in Canada: A Reassessment. *Applied Linguistics* 11 (2): 132–149.

Cutting, J. and Fordyce, K. 2021. *Pragmatics. A Resource Book for Students.* Fourth edition. Abingdon, Oxon: Routledge.

Daloiso, M. 2017. *Supporting Learners with Dyslexia in the ELT Classroom.* Oxford: Oxford University Press.

Deignan, A. 2005. *Metaphor and Corpus Linguistics.* Amsterdam: John Benjamins.

Derwing, T. M. and Munro, M. J. 2005. Second Language Accent and Pronunciation Teaching: A Research-Based Approach. *TESOL Quarterly* 39 (3): 379–397.

Dewaele, J.-M. 2020. What Psychological, Linguistic and Sociobiographical Variables Power EFL/ESL Teachers' Motivation? In C. Gkonou, J.-M. Dewaele and J. King (eds), *The Emotional Rollercoaster of Language Teaching.* Bristol, UK: Multilingual Matters, 269–287.

Dewey, J. 1933. *How We Think: A Re-Statement of the Relation of Reflective Thinking to the Education Process.* Boston, MA: DC Heath & Co.

Domagala-Zyśk, E. and Kontra, E. H. (eds) 2016. *English as a Foreign Language for Deaf and Hard-of-Hearing Persons: Challenges and Strategies.* Newcastle upon Tyne, UK: Cambridge Scholars Publishing.

Dörnyei, Z., Henry, A. and Muir, C. 2016. *Motivational Currents in Language Learning.* Abingdon, Oxon: Routledge.

Dörnyei, Z. and Schmidt, R. 2001. *Motivation and Second Language Acquisition*. University of Hawaii, Manoa: Second Language Teaching & Curriculum Center.

Dudeney, G. and Hockly, N. 2016. Blended Learning in a Mobile Context: New Tools, New Learning Experiences? In M. J. McCarthy (ed.), *The Cambridge Guide to Blended Learning for Language Teaching*. Cambridge: Cambridge University Press, 219–233.

Edge, J. 2002. *Continuing Cooperative Development: A Discourse Framework for Individuals as Colleagues*. Ann Arbor, MI: University of Michigan Press.

Ellis, N. and Wulff, S. 2014. Usage-Based Approaches to SLA. In B. VanPatten and J. Williams (eds), *Theories in Second Language Acquisition*. New York: Routledge, 75–93.

Ellis, R. 1998. Discourse Control and the Acquisition-Rich Classroom. In W. A. Renandya and G. M. Jacobs (eds), *Learners and Language Learning. Anthology Series 39*. Singapore: SEAMO Regional Language Centre, 97–110.

Ellis, R., Basturkmen, H. and Loewen, S. 2001. Preemptive Focus on Form in the ESL Classroom. *TESOL Quarterly* 35 (3): 407–432.

Essen, A. van 2008. Language Awareness and Knowledge about Language: A Historical Overview. In N. H. Hornberger (ed.), *Encyclopedia of Language and Education*. Boston, MA: Springer, 1768–1781.

Evison, J. 2013. A Corpus Linguistic Analysis of Turn-Openings in Spoken Academic Discourse: Understanding Discursive Specialisation. *English Profile Journal* 3 (E4). Available online. doi:10.1017/S2041536212000049.

Eyring, J. L. 2014. Adult Learners in English as a Second/Foreign Language Settings. In M. Celce-Murcia, D. M. Brinton and M. A. Snow (eds), *Teaching English as a Second or Foreign Language*. Fourth edition. Boston, MA: Heinle Cengage Learning/National Geographic Leaning, 568–583.

Farr, F. 2006. Modality in Context: Spoken Language, Variety and the Classroom. In A. Gallagher and M. O. Laoire (eds), *Language Education in Ireland: Current Practice and Future Needs*. Dublin: IRAAL, 165–184.

Farrell, A. 2020. *Corpus Perspectives on the Spoken Models Used by EFL Teachers*. Abingdon, Oxon: Routledge.

Farrell, T. S. C. 2013. *Reflective Writing for Language Teachers*. Sheffield and Bristol, CT: Equinox.

Flowerdew, L. 2013. Needs Analysis and Curriculum Development in ESP. In B. Paltridge and S. Starfield (eds), *The Handbook of English for Specific Purposes*. Oxford: Wiley Blackwell, 325–346.

Freeman, D., Katz, A., Garcia Gomez, P. and Burns, A. 2015. English-for-Teaching: Rethinking Teacher Proficiency in the Classroom. *ELT Journal* 69 (2): 130–139.

Fulcher, G. and Harding, L. 2022. *The Routledge Handbook of Language Testing*. Second edition. Abingdon, Oxon: Routledge.

Gabryś-Barker, D. (ed.) 2018. *Third Age Learners of Foreign Languages*. Bristol: Multilingual Matters.

Gardner, R. C. 2001. Integrative Motivation and Second Language Acquisition. In Z. Dörnyei, and R. Schmidt (eds), *Motivation and Second Language Acquisition*. University of Hawaii, Manoa: Second Language Teaching & Curriculum Center, 1–19.

Genesee, F. 1995. The Canadian Second Language Immersion Program. In O. García and C. Baker (eds), *Policy and Practice in Bilingual Education*. Clevedon: Multilingual Matters Ltd, 118–133.

Gilquin, G. and Granger, S. 2022. Using Data-Driven Learning in Language Teaching. In A. O'Keeffe and M. J. McCarthy (eds), *The Routledge Handbook of Corpus Linguistics*. Second edition. Abingdon, Oxon: Routledge, 430–442.

Grabe, W. and Stoller, F. L. 2018. How Reading Comprehension Works. In J. M. Newton, D. R. Ferris, C. C. M. Goh, W. Grabe, F. L. Stoller and L. Vandergrift (eds), *Teaching English to Second Language Learners in Academic Contexts*. New York: Routledge, 9–27.

Grabe, W. and Yamashita, J. 2022. *Reading in a Second Language: Moving from Theory to Practice*. Second Edition. Cambridge: Cambridge University Press.

Granger, S. Gilquin, G. and Meunier, F. (eds) 2015. *The Cambridge Handbook of Learner Corpus Research*. Cambridge: Cambridge University Press.

Hadley, G. 2002. An Introduction to Data-Driven Learning. *RELC Journal* 33 (2): 99–124.

Hadley, G. and Hadley, H. 2022. Using Research to Inform Materials Development. In J. Norton and H. Buchanan (eds), *The Routledge Handbook of Materials Development in Language Teaching*. Abingdon, Oxon: Routledge, 155–169.

Hafner, C. 2019. Digital Literacies for English Language Learners. In X. Gao (ed.), *Second Handbook of English Language Teaching*. Singapore: Springer International Handbooks of Education, 1–19.

Halliday, M. A. K. 1975. *Learning How to Mean: Explorations in the Development of Language*. London: Edward Arnold.

Halliday, M. A. K. 2014. *Halliday's Introduction to Functional Grammar*. Revised by Christian M. I. M. Matthiessen. Abingdon: Routledge.

Harmer, J. 2004. *How to Teach Writing*. Harlow: Pearson Education Limited.

Harmer, J. 2007. *The Practice of English Language Teaching*. Fourth edition. Harlow: Longman.

Harrington, K. 2022. *The Role of Corpus Linguistics in the Ethnography of a Closed Community: Survival Communication*. Abingdon, Oxon: Routledge.

Hinkel, E. 2006. Perspectives on Teaching the Four Skills. *TESOL Quarterly* 40 (1): 109–131.

Hobbs, V. 2007. Faking It or Hating It: Can Reflective Practice Be Forced? *Reflective Practice* 8 (3): 405–417.

Hoey, M. 2001. *Textual Interaction: An Introduction to Written Discourse Analysis*. Abingdon: Routledge.

Hofstadter, D. 1995. *Fluid Concepts & Creative Analogies: Computer Models of the Fundamental Mechanisms of Thought*. New York: Basic Books.

Hudson, T. 2007. *Teaching Second Language Reading*. Oxford: Oxford University Press.

Hulstijn, J. H. 2013. Incidental Learning in Second Language Acquisition. In C. A. Chapelle (ed.), *The Encyclopedia of Applied Linguistics*. Volume 5. Oxford: Wiley-Blackwell, 2632–2640.

Hunston, S. and Francis, G. 2000. *Pattern Grammar: A Corpus-Driven Approach to the Lexical Grammar of English*. Amsterdam: John Benjamins.

Hyland, K. 2019. *Second Language Writing*. Second edition. Cambridge: Cambridge University Press.

Hymes, D. 1972. On Communicative Competence. In J. B. Pride and J. Holmes (eds), *Sociolinguistics: Selected Readings*. Harmondsworth: Penguin, 269–293.

Johnson, K. E. 2009. *Second Language Teacher Education: A Sociocultural Perspective*. New York: Routledge.

Johnson, K. E. and Golombek, P. (eds) 2011. *Research on Second Language Teacher Education: A Sociocultural Perspective on Professional Development*. New York: Routledge.

Jones, C. 2022. Authenticity in Language Teaching Materials. In J. Norton and H. Buchanan (eds), *The Routledge Handbook of Materials Development in Language Teaching*. Abingdon, Oxon: Routledge, 65–77.

Kecskes, I. 2019. *English as a Lingua Franca: The Pragmatic Perspective*. Cambridge: Cambridge University Press.

Kelly, G. 2000. *How to Teach Pronunciation*. Harlow: Longman.

Kemmis, S. and McTaggart, R. 1988. *The Action Research Planner*. Melbourne: Deakin University Press.

Kennedy, A. 2011. Collaborative Continuing Professional Development (CPD) for Teachers in Scotland: Aspirations, Opportunities and Barriers. *European Journal of Teacher Education* 34 (1): 25–41.

Klein, P. D. 1997. Multiplying the Problems of Intelligence by Eight: A Critique of Gardner's Theory. *Canadian Journal of Education / Revue canadienne de l'éducation* 22 (4): 377–394.

Knowles, G. 2014. *Patterns of Spoken English: An Introduction to English Phonetics*. Abingdon, Oxon: Routledge.

Kohnke, L. and Moorhouse, B. L. 2020. Facilitating Synchronous Online Language Learning through Zoom. *RELC Journal* 53 (1): 296–301.

Kormos, J. 2020. Specific Learning Difficulties in Second Language Learning and Teaching. *Language Teaching* 53 (2): 129–143.

Kramsch, C. 1986. From Language Proficiency to Interactional Competence. *The Modern Language Journal* 70 (4): 366–372.

Krashen, S. 1994. The Input Hypothesis and Its Rivals. In N. C. Ellis (ed.), *Implicit and Explicit Learning of Languages*. London: Academic Press, 45–77.

Kumaravadivelu, B. 2001. Toward a Postmethod Pedagogy. *TESOL Quarterly* 35 (4): 537–560.

Kumaravadivelu, B. 2003. *Beyond Methods: Macrostrategies for Language Teaching*. New Haven: Yale University Press.

Labov, W. 1972. *Language in the Inner City*. Philadelphia. University of Pennsylvania Press.

Lantolf, J. P. 2000. *Sociocultural Theory and Second Language Learning*. Oxford: Oxford University Press.

Larsen-Freeman, D. 2003. *Teaching Language: From Grammar to Grammaring*. Boston, MA: Heinle.

Latham-Koenig, C., Oxenden, C. and Chomacki, K. 2020. *English File Upper-Intermediate Student's Book*. Fourth Edition. Oxford: Oxford University Press.

Laufer, B. 1997. What's in a Word That Makes It Hard or Easy: Some Intralexical Features That Affect the Learning of Words. In N. Schmitt and M. J. McCarthy (eds), *Vocabulary: Description, Acquisition and Pedagogy*. Cambridge: Cambridge University Press, 140–155.

Laufer, B. 2013. Lexical Thresholds for Reading Comprehension: What They Are and How They Can Be Used for Teaching Purposes. *TESOL Quarterly* 47 (4): 867–872.

Lazaraton, A. 2014. Second Language Speaking. In M. Celce-Murcia, D. M. Brinton and M. A. Snow (eds), *Teaching English as a Second or Foreign Language*. Fourth edition. Boston, MA: Heinle Cengage Learning/National Geographic Leaning, 106–135.

Leung, C. 2005. Convivial Communication: Recontextualizing Communicative Competence. *International Journal of Applied Linguistics* 15 (2): 119–144.

Lillie, K. E., Markos, A., Arias, M. B. and Wiley, T. G. 2012. Separate and Not Equal: The Implementation of Structured English Immersion in Arizona's Classrooms. *Teachers College Record* 114 (9): 1–33.

Littlejohn, A. 2022. The Analysis and Evaluation of Language Teaching Materials. In J. Norton and H. Buchanan (eds), *The Routledge Handbook of Materials Development in Language Teaching*. Abingdon, Oxon: Routledge, 263–276.

Liu, Y. 2014. Perceived Problems of Novice English as a Foreign Language Teachers in Taiwan. *International Journal on Studies in English Language and Literature (IJSELL)* 2 (5): 41–45.

Llurda, E. 2016. 'Native Speakers', English and ELT. In G. Hall (ed.), *The Routledge Handbook of English Language Teaching*. Abingdon, Oxon: Routledge, 51–63.

Long, M. H. 1983. Native Speaker/Non-Native Speaker Conversation and the Negotiation of Meaning. *Applied Linguistics* 4 (2): 126–141.

Lu, X. 2010. Automatic Analysis of Syntactic Complexity in Second Language Writing. *International Journal of Corpus Linguistics* 15 (4): 474–496.

Lyle, J. 2003. Stimulated Recall: A Report on Its Use in Naturalistic Research. *British Educational Research Journal* 29 (6): 861–878.

Macaro, E. 2018. *English Medium Instruction.* Oxford: Oxford University Press.

Mann, S. 2016. *The Research Interview: Reflective Practice and Reflexivity in Research Processes.* London: Springer.

Mann, S. and Walsh, S. 2013. RP or 'RIP': A Critical Perspective on Reflective Practice. *Applied Linguistics Review* 4 (2): 291–315.

Mann, S. and Walsh, S. 2017. *Reflective Practice in English Language Teaching: Research-Based Principles and Practices.* New York: Routledge.

Mauranen, A., Hynninen, N. and Ranta, E. 2016. English as the Academic Lingua Franca. In K. Hyland and P. Shaw (eds), *The Routledge Handbook of English for Academic Purposes.* Abingdon, Oxon: Routledge, 44–55.

McCabe, M., Walsh, S., Wideman, R. and Winter, E. 2009. The 'R Word' in Teacher Education: Understanding the Teaching and Learning of Critical Reflective Practice. *International Electronic Journal for Leadership in Learning* 13 (7): 1–14.

McCarten, J. 2007. *Teaching Vocabulary: Lessons from the Corpus, Lessons for the Classroom.* Cambridge: Cambridge University Press.

McCarthy, M. J. 1998. *Spoken Language and Applied Linguistics.* Cambridge: Cambridge University Press.

McCarthy, M. J. 2002. Good Listenership Made Plain: British and American Non-Minimal Response Tokens in Everyday Conversation. In R. Reppen, S. Fitzmaurice and D. Biber (eds), *Using Corpora to Explore Linguistic Variation.* Amsterdam: John Benjamins, 49–71.

McCarthy, M. J. 2010a. The Festival Incident. In D. Nunan and J. Choi (eds), *Language and Culture.* New York and London: Routledge, 140–146.

McCarthy, M. J. 2010b. Spoken Fluency Revisited. *English Profile Journal* 1 (E4). Available online: doi:10.1017/S2041536210000012.

McCarthy, M. J. 2013. Corpora and the Advanced Level: Problems and Prospects. *English Australia Journal* 29 (1): 39–49.

McCarthy, M. J. 2015. The Role of Corpus Research in the Design of Advanced Level Grammar Instruction. In M. A. Christison, D. Christian, P. A. Duff, & N. Spada (eds), *Teaching and Learning English Grammar: Research Findings and Future Directions.* New York, NY: Routledge, 87–102.

McCarthy, M. J. 2016a. Teaching Grammar at the Advanced Level. In E. Hinkel (ed.), *Teaching English Grammar to Speakers of Other Languages.* New York: Routledge, 203–221.

McCarthy, M. J. (ed.) 2016b. *The Cambridge Guide to Blended Learning for Language Teaching.* Cambridge: Cambridge University Press.

McCarthy, M. J. 2023. *English Vocabulary: The Basics*. Abingdon, Oxon: Routledge.

McCarthy, M. J. and Clancy, B. 2019. From Language as System to Language as Discourse. In S. Walsh and S. Mann (eds), *The Routledge Handbook of English Language Teacher Education*. London: Routledge, 201–215.

McCarthy, M. J. and McCarten, J. 2018. Now You're Talking! Practising Conversation in Second Language Learning. In C. Jones (ed.), *Practice in Second Language Learning*. Cambridge: Cambridge University Press, 7–29.

McCarthy, M. J. and McCarten, J. 2023. Speaking and Listening: Two Sides of the Same Coin. In K. Harrington and P. Ronan (eds), *Demystifying Corpus Linguistics for English Language Teaching*. Basingstoke, Hants: Palgrave Macmillan, 59–77.

McCarthy, M. J., McCarten, J. and Sandiford, H. 2005. *Touchstone*. Student's Book 1. Cambridge: Cambridge University Press.

McCarthy, M. J., McCarten, J. and Sandiford, H. 2012. *Viewpoint*. Student's Book 1. Cambridge: Cambridge University Press.

McCarthy, M. J., McCarten, J. and Sandiford, H. 2014a. *Touchstone*. Second edition. Student's Book 1. Cambridge: Cambridge University Press.

McCarthy, M. J., McCarten, J. and Sandiford, H. 2014b. *Viewpoint*. Student's Book 2. Cambridge: Cambridge University Press.

McCarthy, M. J. and O'Dell, F. 2017a. *English Phrasal Verbs in Use: Intermediate*. Second edition. Cambridge: Cambridge University Press.

McCarthy, M. J. and O'Dell, F. 2017b. *English Collocations in Use: Advanced*. Second edition. Cambridge: Cambridge University Press.

McCarthy, M. J. and O'Dell, F. 2017c. *English Idioms in Use: Intermediate*. Second edition. Cambridge: Cambridge University Press.

McCarthy, M. J. and Walsh, S. 2003. Discourse. In D. Nunan (ed.), *Practical English Language Teaching*. San Francisco: McGraw-Hill, 28–54.

Mercer, N. 2008. Why Classroom Dialogue Needs a Temporal Analysis. *Journal of the Learning Sciences* 17 (1): 33–59.

Merrill, D. C., Reiser, B. J., Merrill, S. K. and Landes, S. 1995. Tutoring: Guided Learning by Doing. *Cognition and Instruction* 13 (3): 315–372.

Moorhouse, B. L. 2020. Adaptations to a Face-to-Face Initial Teacher Education Course 'Forced' Online Due to the COVID-19 Pandemic. *Journal of Education for Teaching* 46 (4): 609–611.

Moorhouse, B., Li, Y. and Walsh, S. 2021. E-Classroom Interactional Competencies: Mediating and Assisting Language Learning During Synchronous Online Lessons. *RELC Journal* 52 (3): 359–378.

Muñoz, C. (ed.) 2006. *Age and the Rate of Foreign Language Learning*. Clevedon: Multilingual Matters.

Myles, F. 2015. Second Language Acquisition Theory and Learner Corpus Research. In S. Granger, G. Gilquin and F. Meunier (eds), *The Cambridge*

Handbook of Learner Corpus Research. Cambridge: Cambridge University Press, 309–332.

Nahal, S. P. 2010. Voices from the Field: Perspectives of First-Year Teachers on the Disconnect between Teacher Preparation Programs and the Realities of the Classroom. *The International Journal of Research in Teacher Education* 51 (1): 2–19.

Nation, I. S. P. 1990. *Teaching and Learning Vocabulary*. New York: Newbury House.

Nation, I. S. P. and Coxhead, A. 2021. *Measuring Native-Speaker Vocabulary Size*. Amsterdam: John Benjamins.

Nation, I. S. P. and Macalister, J. 2021. *Teaching ESL/EFL Reading and Writing*. Second edition. New York: Routledge.

Nation, I. S. P. and Waring, R. 1997. Vocabulary Size, Text Coverage and Word Lists. In N. Schmitt and M. J. McCarthy (eds), *Vocabulary: Description, Acquisition and Pedagogy*. Cambridge: Cambridge University Press, 6–19.

Newton, M. J. and Nation, I. S. P. 2020. *Teaching ESL/EFL Listening and Speaking*. Second Edition. New York: Routledge.

Nickerson, C. 2005. English as a *Lingua Franca* in International Business Contexts. *English for Specific Purposes* 24 (4): 367–380.

Norton, B. 2011. Identity. In J. Simpson (ed.), *The Routledge Handbook of Applied Linguistics*. Abingdon, Oxon: Routledge, 318–330.

O'Keeffe, A. and Adolphs, S. 2008. Response tokens in British and Irish English. In K. P. Schneider and A. Barron (eds), *Variational Pragmatics*. Amsterdam: John Benjamins, 69–98.

O'Keeffe, A., Clancy, B. and Adolphs, S. 2020. *Introducing Pragmatics in Use*. Second edition. Abingdon, Oxon: Routledge.

O'Keeffe, A. and Mark, G. 2017. The English Grammar Profile of Learner Competence. *International Journal of Corpus Linguistics* 22 (4): 457–489.

O'Keeffe, A. and McCarthy, M. J. (eds) 2022. *The Routledge Handbook of Corpus Linguistics*. Second edition. Abingdon, Oxon: Routledge.

O'Keeffe, A., McCarthy, M. J. and Carter, R. 2007. *From Corpus to Classroom*. Cambridge: Cambridge University Press.

Paltridge, B. 2022. *Discourse Analysis: An Introduction*. Third edition. London: Bloomsbury Academic.

Paltridge, B. and Starfield, S. (eds) 2013. *The Handbook of English for Specific Purposes*. Oxford: Wiley Blackwell.

Payne, J. S. 2020. Developing L2 Productive Language Skills Online and the Strategic Use of Instructional Tools. *Foreign Language Annals* 53 (2): 243–249.

Peachey, N. 2017. Synchronous Online Teaching. In In M. Carrier, R. M. Damerow and K. M. Bailey (eds), *Digital Language Learning and Teaching*. New York: Routledge, 143–155.

Pérez-Paredes, P. 2022. A Systematic Review of the Uses and Spread of Corpora and Data-Driven Learning in CALL Research During 2011–2015. *Computer Assisted Language Learning* 35 (1–2): 36–61.

Perfetti, C. and Harris, L. 2017. Learning to Read English. In L. Verhoeven and C. Perfetti (eds), *Learning to Read across Languages and Writing Systems*. Cambridge: Cambridge University Press, 347–370.

Peterson, E. 2020. *Making Sense of 'Bad English': An Introduction to Language Attitudes and Ideologies*. Abingdon, Oxon: Routledge.

Pfenninger, S. E. and Polz, S. 2018. Foreign Language Learning in the Third Age: A Pilot Feasibility Study on Cognitive, Socio-Affective and Linguistic Drivers and Benefits in Relation to Previous Bilingualism of the Learner. *Journal of the European Second Language Association* 2 (1): 1–13.

Puchta, H., Stranks, J. and Lewis-Jones, P. 2022. *Think*. Level 2 Student's book. Second edition. Cambridge: Cambridge University Press.

Qian, D. 2002. Investigating the Relationship between Vocabulary Knowledge and Academic Reading Performance: An Assessment Perspective. *Language Learning* 52 (3): 513–536.

Racine, J. P. 2018. Lexical Approach. In J. I. Liontas (ed.), *The TESOL Encyclopedia of English Language Teaching*. First edition. Volume II. Hoboken, NJ: John Wiley and Sons, Inc., 1–7.

Rassaei, E. 2014. Scaffolded Feedback, Recasts, and L2 Development: A Sociocultural Perspective. *The Modern Language Journal* 98 (1): 417–431.

Rehn, N., Maor, D. and McConney, A. 2018. The Specific Skills Required of Teachers Who Deliver K-12 Distance Education Courses by Synchronous Videoconference: Implications for Training and Professional Development. *Technology, Pedagogy and Education* 27 (4): 417–429.

Richards, J. C. 2015. *Key Issues in Language Teaching*. Cambridge: Cambridge University Press.

Richards, J. C. and Rodgers, T. S. 2001. *Approaches and Methods in Language Teaching*. Second edition. Cambridge: Cambridge University Press.

Roach, P. 2001. *Phonetics*. Oxford: Oxford University Press.

Roberts, J. 1998. *Language Teacher Education*. London: Arnold.

Rőmer, U. and Garner, J. 2022. What Can Corpus Linguistics Tell Us about Second Language Acquisition. In In A. O'Keeffe and M. J. McCarthy (eds), *The Routledge Handbook of Corpus Linguistics*. Second edition. Abingdon, Oxon: Routledge, 328–340.

Rost, M. 2001. Listening. In R. Carter and D. Nunan (eds), *The Cambridge Guide to Teaching English to Speakers of Other Languages*. Cambridge: Cambridge University Press, 7–13.

Rubin, J. 1975. What the 'Good Language Learner Can Teach Us'. *TESOL Quarterly* 9 (1): 41–51.

Rühlemann, C. and Schweinberger, M. 2021. Which Word Gets the Nuclear Stress in a Turn-at-Talk? *Journal of Pragmatics* 178: 426–439.

Sarner, M. 2022. When I Grow Up. *New Scientist* 12 November: 40–43.

Sato, R. 2010. Reconsidering the Effectiveness and Suitability of PPP and TBLT in the Japanese EFL Classroom. *JALT Journal* 32 (2): 189–200.

Saville, N. 2017. Digital Assessment. In M. Carrier, R. M. Damerow and K. M. Bailey (eds), *Digital Language Learning and Teaching*. New York: Routledge, 198–207.

Schmidt, R. 1990. The Role of Consciousness in Second Language Learning. *Applied Linguistics* 11: 129–158.

Schmidt, R. 1993. Awareness and Second Language Acquisition. *Annual Review of Applied Linguistics* 13: 206–226.

Schmitt, N. 1997. Vocabulary Learning Strategies. In N. Schmitt and M. J. McCarthy (eds), *Vocabulary: Description, Acquisition and Pedagogy*. Cambridge: Cambridge University Press, 199–227.

Schmitt, N. (ed.) 2004. *Formulaic Sequences*. Amsterdam: John Benjamins.

Schmitt, N., Jiang, X. and Grabe, W. 2011. The Percentage of Words Known in a Text and Reading Comprehension. *The Modern Language Journal* 95 (1): 26–43.

Schmitt, N. and Schmitt, D. 2014. A Reassessment of Frequency and Vocabulary Size in L2 Vocabulary Teaching. *Language Teaching* 47 (4): 484–503.

Schneider, E. W. 2020. *English Around the World: An Introduction*. Second edition. Cambridge: Cambridge University Press.

Schön, D. 1991. *The Reflective Practitioner*. Aldershot: Ashgate Publishing Ltd.

Scrivener, J. 2011. *Learning Teaching*. Third Edition. Oxford: Macmillan Education.

Seedhouse, P. 1997. The Case of the Missing 'No': The Relationship between Pedagogy and Interaction. *Language Learning* 47 (3): 547–583.

Seedhouse, P. 2004. *The Interactional Architecture of the Second Language Classroom: A Conversational Analysis Perspective*. Oxford: Blackwell.

Seedhouse, P. 2022. (ed.) *Video Enhanced Observation for Language Teaching: Reflection and Professional Development*. London: Bloomsbury.

Seidlhofer, B. 2001. Pronunciation. In R. Carter and D. Nunan (eds), *The Cambridge Guide to Teaching English to Speakers of Other Languages*. Cambridge: Cambridge University Press, 56–65.

Selinker, L. 1972. Interlanguage. *IRAL (International Review of Applied Linguistics)* 10 (1–4): 209–232.

Selvi, A. F. 2019. The Non-Native Teacher. In S. Walsh and S. Mann (eds), *The Routledge Handbook of English Language Teacher Education*. Abingdon, Oxon: Routledge, 184–194.

Shin, J. K. 2014. Teaching Young Learners in English as a Second/Foreign Language Settings. In M. Celce-Murcia, D. M. Brinton and M. A. Snow (eds),

Teaching English as a Second or Foreign Language. Fourth edition. Boston, MA: Heinle Cengage Learning/National Geographic Leaning, 550–567.

Sinclair, J. McH. and Coulthard, R. M. 1975. *Towards an Analysis of Discourse.* London: Oxford University Press.

Singleton, D. 2001. Age and Second Language Acquisition. *Annual Review of Applied Linguistics* 21: 77–89.

Skehan, P. 1998. *A Cognitive Approach to Language Learning.* Oxford: Oxford University Press.

Slimani, A. 1992. The Role of Topicalization in Classroom Language Learning. *System* 17: 223–234.

Sparkes, M. 2023. Searching for Answers. *New Scientist* 257 (3247): 12–13.

Stenström, A.-B., Andersen, G. and Hasund, I. K. 2002. *Trends in Teenage Talk: Corpus Compilation, Analysis and Findings.* Amsterdam: John Benjamins.

Stickler, U. 2022. *Technology and Language Teaching.* Cambridge: Cambridge University Press.

Summer, T. 2012. Introduction: From Method to Postmethod. In M. Eisenmann and T. Summer (eds), *Basic Issues in EFL Teaching and Learning.* Heidelberg: Universitätsverlag Winter, 1–15.

Swain, M. 2000. The Output Hypothesis and Beyond: Mediating Acquisition through Collaborative Dialogue. In J. P. Lantolf (ed.), *Sociocultural Theory and Second Language Learning.* Oxford: Oxford University Press, 97–114.

Swan, M. 2005. Legislation by Hypothesis: The Case of Task-Based Instruction. *Applied Linguistics* 26 (3): 376–401.

Swan, M. and Smith, B. 2001. *Learner English: A Teacher's Guide to Interference and Other Problems.* Second edition. Cambridge: Cambridge University Press.

Szudarski, P. 2018. *Corpus Linguistics for Vocabulary.* Abingdon, Oxon: Routledge.

Taguchi, N. 2014. English-Medium Education in the Global Society: Introduction to the Special Issue. *International Review of Applied Linguistics in Language Teaching* 52 (2): 89–98.

Taylor-Leech, K. and Yates, L. 2012. Strategies for Building Social Connection through English: Challenges for Immigrants and Implications for Teaching English as a Second Language. *Australian Review of Applied Linguistics* 35 (2): 138–155.

Thornbury, S. 1999. *How to Teach Grammar.* Harlow: Longman.

Thornbury, S. 2002. *How to Teach Vocabulary.* Harlow: Longman.

Thornbury, S. 2011. Language Teaching Methodology. In J. Simpson (ed.), *The Routledge Handbook of Applied Linguistics.* Abingdon, Oxon: Routledge, 185–199.

Timmis, I. 2022. Theory and Practice in Materials Development. In J. Norton and H. Buchanan (eds), *The Routledge Handbook of Materials Development in Language Teaching.* Abingdon, Oxon: Routledge, 30–46.

Toledo-Sandoval, F. 2020. Local Culture and Locally Produced ELT Textbooks: How Do Teachers Bridge the Gap? *System* 95: 102362.

Tolson, A. 2010. A New Authenticity? Communicative Practices on YouTube. *Critical Discourse Studies* 7 (4): 277–289.

Torff, B. and Gardner, H. 1999. The Vertical Mind – The Case for Multiple Intelligences. In M. Anderson (ed.), *The Development of Intelligence*. Hove: Psychology Press Ltd, 139–159.

Turan, Z. and Akdag-Cimen, B. 2020. Flipped Classroom in English Language Teaching: A Systematic Review. *Computer Assisted Language Learning* 33 (5–6): 590–606.

Tyen, G., Brenchley, M., Caines, A. and Buttery, P. 2022a. Towards an Open-Domain Chatbot for Language Practice. In *Proceedings of the 17th Workshop on Innovative Use of NLP for Building Educational Applications (BEA 2022)*. Seattle, Washington: Association for Computational Linguistics, 234–249.

Tyen, G., Brenchley, M., Caines, A. and Buttery, P. 2022b. A Chatbot for Learners of English as a Foreign Language. *Paper Presented at the TaLC Conference*, University of Limerick, Ireland, 14 July 2022.

Ur, P. 2012. *A Course in English Language Teaching*. Second edition. Cambridge: Cambridge University Press.

Ur, P. 2013. Language-Teaching Method Revisited. *ELT Journal* 67 (4): 468–474.

Valente, D. and Xerri, D. (eds) 2022. *Innovative Practices in Early English Language Education*. Cham: Springer Nature Switzerland AG.

Vanderplank, R. 2010. Déjà vu? A Decade of Research on Language Laboratories, Television and Video in Language Learning. *Language Teaching* 43 (1): 1–37.

Van Lier, L. 1988. *The Classroom and the Language Learner*. London: Longman.

Van Lier, L. 2010. The Ecology of Language Learning: Practice to Theory, Theory to Practice. *Procedia: Social and Behavioural Sciences* 3: 2–6.

VanPatten, B., Keating, G. D. and Wulff, S. (eds) 2020. *Theories in Second Language Acquisition*. New York: Routledge, 1–18.

Vercellotti, M. L. 2017. The Development of Complexity, Accuracy, and Fluency in Second Language Performance: A Longitudinal Study. *Applied Linguistics* 38 (1): 90–111.

Viana, V. and O'Boyle, A. 2022. *Corpus Linguistics for English for Academic Purposes*. Abingdon, Oxon: Routledge.

Walsh, S. 2002. Construction or Obstruction: Teacher Talk and Learner Involvement in the EFL Classroom. *Language Teaching Research* 6 (1): 3–23.

Walsh, S. 2006. *Investigating Classroom Discourse*. Abingdon, Oxon: Routledge.

Walsh, S. 2011. *Exploring Classroom Discourse: Language in Action*. Abingdon, Oxon: Routledge.

Walsh, S. 2013. *Classroom Discourse and Teacher Development*. Edinburgh: Edinburgh University Press.

Walsh, S. 2014. *Classroom Interaction for Language Teachers*. Alexandria, VA: TESOL Press.

Walsh, S. 2019. SETTVEO: Evidence-Based Reflection and Teacher Development. *ELT Research Papers* 19 (5): 3–24.

Walsh, S. and Li, L. 2013. Conversations as Space for Learning. *International Journal of Applied Linguistics* 23 (2): 247–266.

Walsh, S. and Mann, S. 2015. Doing Reflective Practice: A Data-Led Way Forward. *ELT Journal* 69 (4): 351–362.

Walsh, S., and O'Keeffe, A. 2007. Applying CA to a Modes Analysis of Third Level Spoken Academic Discourse. In H. Bowles and P. Seedhouse (eds), *Conversation Analysis and Languages for Specific Purposes*. Bern: Peter Lang, 101–139.

Waring, H. Z. 2013. Two Mentor Practices that Generate Teacher Reflection without Explicit Solicitations: Some Preliminary Considerations. *RELC Journal* 44 (1): 103–119.

Wenlock, R. 1937. *Preparatory English Course for Foreign Students*. London: Macmillan and Co. Ltd.

White, J. 2006. The Trouble with Multiple Intelligences. *Teaching Geography* 31 (2): 82–83.

Wilkins, A. 2023. A Robotic Personality. *New Scientist* 257 (3431): 28.

Wilkins, D. 1976a. *Notional Syllabuses*. London: Oxford University Press.

Wilkins, D. 1976b. Notional Syllabuses: Theory into Practice. *Bulletin CILA* (Commission interuniversitaire suisse de linguistique appliquée) 24: 5–17.

Willis, D. 1990. *The Lexical Syllabus*. London: Collins ELT.

Willis, D. and Willis, J. 2001. Task-Based Language Learning. In R. Carter and D. Nunan (eds), *The Cambridge Guide to Teaching English to Speakers of Other Languages*. Cambridge: Cambridge University Press, 173–179.

Winter, J. 2002. Discourse Quotatives in Australian English: Adolescents Performing Voices. *Australian Journal of Linguistics* 22 (1): 5–21.

Wolter, B. 2001. Comparing the L1 and L2 Mental Lexicon: A Depth of Individual Word Knowledge Model. *Studies in Second Language Acquisition* 23 (1): 41–69.

Yang, H., Kim, H., Lee, J. and Shin, D. 2022. Implementation of an AI Chatbot as an English Conversation Partner in EFL Speaking Classes. *ReCALL* 34 (3): 327–343.

Zacarian, D. 2021. *TESOL Zip Guide: Social-Emotional Learning for English Learners*. Alexandria, VA: TESOL Press.

INDEX

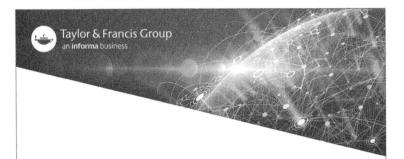